# THE MILLIONAIRE UPSTAIRS

UNLOCK YOUR WEALTHY MIND THROUGH GROWING YOUR MONEY, FINANCIAL LITERACY, AND INVESTING FOR ADULTS

YOU WILL ROCK BOOKS

# CONTENTS

# INTRODUCTION

## The True Mathematics of Wealth

Money has rules. Not the kind you learned in school, not the kind your parents whispered about over bills at the kitchen table, but real rules, as reliable as gravity and just as powerful when you understand how to use them.

Right now, someone with less talent than you is building wealth. Someone with fewer advantages is watching their money multiply. Someone who started with nothing is on track to retire early. The difference between them and everyone else isn't luck, inheritance, or some secret the rich refuse to share. It's understanding how money actually works, and more importantly, doing something about it.

Here's what nobody tells you: building wealth is boring in the same way brushing your teeth is boring, simple, repetitive, but life-changing if you do it consistently. In fact, it's so boring that most people would rather stay broke than follow the simple steps that virtually guarantee financial success. There's no drama in automatic transfers to investment accounts. No excitement in spending less than you earn. No social media moments in saying no to the car you can't afford. But while everyone else chases the next hot stock tip or cryptocurrency moonshot, the boring people quietly become millionaires.

The system is hiding in plain sight. It's in every success story you've heard but dismissed as being "irrelevant" to your situation. It's in the retirement accounts of ordinary teachers and mechanics who somehow retired as millionaires. It's about a small business owner who started with nothing and built an empire. The pattern is always the same, the principles never change, yet most people spend their entire lives never seeing it.

Think about this: every morning, millions of people wake up, go to work, collect a paycheck, and wonder why they're not getting ahead. They're smart people, doctors, engineers, managers, skilled professionals, yet they live paycheck to paycheck. Meanwhile, someone making half their salary is building wealth. The difference isn't the amount of money coming in. It's what happens to that money once it arrives.

Our education system will teach you calculus but not compound interest. You'll learn to analyze Shakespeare but not a financial statement. You can recite historical dates but not the basic formula for building wealth. This isn't an accident. A system that depends on consumers needs people who consume, not people who accumulate. It needs workers, not owners. It needs borrowers, not lenders.

But what if you could flip the script? What if instead of being the person paying interest, you became the person earning it? Instead of making someone else rich, you made yourself wealthy? Instead of hoping for financial security, you could mathematically guarantee it?

Consider this book your blueprint for that transformation. Not through motivational speeches or wishful thinking, but through understanding and applying principles that work as reliably as physics. You'll discover why some people seem to attract money effortlessly while others repel it despite working twice as hard. You'll learn why the "smart" financial decisions you've been taught might be keeping you poor. And most importantly, you'll get a step-by-step system you can start implementing today, regardless of where you're starting from.

The wealthy aren't smarter than you. They aren't luckier than you. And despite what hustle culture says, many of them actually work less than you. They simply understand truths about money that seem almost magical to everyone else but are actually just mathematics. Truths like how a small amount invested consistently becomes a fortune. How eliminating certain expenses can make you rich. How some assets feed you while others eat you. How time can be your greatest ally or your worst enemy, depending on which side of the equation you're on.

Every chapter in this book builds on a simple premise: if you understand the rules, you can win the game. Not might win, not could win, but will win, as surely as dropping a ball means it will hit the ground. The principles don't care about your past mistakes, your current situation, or your education level. They work for anyone who applies them, and they fail for anyone who doesn't.

You'll learn about modern wealth accelerators that didn't exist for your parents' generation, tools that can compress decades of wealth building into years. Digital businesses that scale infinitely. Investment platforms that cost nothing. Income streams you can create from your phone. Geographic arbitrage that lets you earn in strong currencies while spending in weak ones. These aren't get-rich-quick schemes, they're get-rich-quicker realities when combined with timeless principles.

But here's the beautiful truth: you don't need all of it. You don't need to become a real estate mogul or start the next tech unicorn. You don't need to time the market perfectly or pick winning stocks. You just need to understand and apply a handful of principles consistently. Do that, and wealth becomes not a possibility but an inevitability.

The journey ahead will challenge everything you think you know about money. It will reveal why the financial advice you've been following might be designed to keep you dependent rather than free. It will show you opportunities hiding in plain sight and dangers disguised as common sense. Most importantly, it will give you a clear, actionable path from wherever you are now to wherever you want to be financially.

This isn't about sacrifice or deprivation. It's about designing a life where money works for you instead of you working for money. Where your wealth grows while you sleep. Where financial stress becomes a distant memory. Where you have the freedom to make choices based on what you want, not what you can afford.

The math is simple. The principles are proven. The only question is whether you're ready to stop hoping and start knowing. Whether you're willing to be bored in exchange for being wealthy. Whether you can ignore what everyone else is doing long enough to get what everyone else wants.

Turn the page, and let's begin. Your financial transformation starts with the next chapter, but it starts with a decision you make right now. The decision to stop being a victim of money and start being its master. The formulas are waiting. The system is ready. All that's missing is you.

**Bonus**

As a way of saying *thank you* for investing in this book, and for choosing to think differently about money, we're including an exclusive bonus resource designed to help you move from insight to action.

Understanding the rules of money is powerful. Applying them is what changes everything. This bonus exists to help bridge that gap by giving you practical tools you can use immediately, without complexity or guesswork.

**Inside this resource, you'll find:**

• Key money rules most people never learn, and how to apply them in real life

• Common financial mistakes that quietly keep people stuck (and how to avoid them)

• Small habit shifts that compound into massive financial results over time

• Clear next steps you can take right now, regardless of your current income or starting point

**Scan the QR code below** to unlock your exclusive bonus resource and start putting the rules of money to work for you today.

## 1

### THE FOUNDATION OF
### MONEY AND WEALTH

Money is stored energy and crystallized time, a tool that can work even when you aren't. Every dollar you possess represents a claim on future goods and services. When you work, you convert time and energy into these claims. When you spend, you exchange these claims for immediate consumption. But when you invest, something transformative happens: your claims start generating their own claims.

This is the fundamental difference between the wealthy and everyone else. The wealthy understand that money can work harder and longer than any human ever could.

Consider the mathematics:

- If you work 40 hours per week for 50 weeks per year, you're working 2,000 hours annually.
- Even working every waking hour would max out at around 5,840 hours per year.
- Money invested in the stock market works 8,760 hours per year, every single hour of every single day.

- It doesn't need sleep, vacations, sick days, or coffee breaks.
- It has no maximum hours and never burns out.

The transformation from laborer to capitalist happens when your money starts making money. This progression follows a predictable pattern. First, you trade time for money through employment. Then you save money from that time exchange. Finally, that saved money generates returns, creating money from money rather than from time. This transition marks the beginning of true wealth building. Each dollar invested becomes a tiny employee working for you forever, and unlike human employees, these dollar employees work for free, never complain, and multiply over time.

Think of it this way: when you buy a stock, you're purchasing a tiny slice of a company with thousands of employees, billions in assets, and decades of expertise. All of that works for you while you sleep, play, or pursue other interests. This is leverage at its finest, using other people's time, energy, and expertise to build your wealth.

## The Parable of Two Brothers

Two brothers inherited $50,000 each from their grandmother in 1990.

The first brother, thinking himself prudent, put every penny in savings accounts and CDs. "Safe and secure," he told everyone. "Grandma would be proud." By 2024, his $50,000 had grown to $95,000, nearly doubled! But when he went to buy a modest house in his hometown, he discovered that the $100,000 homes from 1990 now cost $400,000. His "safe" money had actually lost three-quarters of its purchasing power.

The second brother invested in a simple S&P 500 index fund and forgot about it. No trading, no timing, no cleverness, just ownership of American businesses. By 2024, his $50,000 had become $1.2 million. While his brother struggled with a down payment, he bought his house with cash.

The difference wasn't intelligence or luck. One brother saved currency that was designed to lose value. The other owned assets that grew with the economy. One worked for money. The other made money work for them.

This same story plays out millions of times across America, in break rooms where colleagues compare 401(k)s to savings accounts, in retirement homes where some worry about every expense while others live comfortably, in families where financial wisdom either was or wasn't passed down.

## The Modern Monetary System

In 1971, the U.S. dollar severed its final link to gold. From that moment on, money was no longer tied to a physical asset, it became a policy decision. Governments and central banks gained the ability to create new dollars as needed, without the limitation of hard assets backing them.

For governments and central banks, that flexibility is powerful. For everyday earners and savers, it introduces a quiet problem. When new money is created faster than real value is produced, each dollar buys a little less than it used to. You don't notice it week to week, but over years, it reshapes your financial outcomes.

That change rewrote the rules of wealth building. In an economy designed around expanding money supply, simply saving cash no longer preserves value. Today, central banks influence the economy through money creation, using mechanisms such as:

- **Quantitative easing** - Direct purchase of bonds and assets with newly created money.
- **Open market operations** - Buying and selling government securities to influence money supply.
- **Adjusting reserve requirements** - Changing how much banks must hold versus lend
- **Setting interest rates** - Influencing the cost of borrowing and saving throughout the economy.

This money creation causes inflation, the silent tax that erodes purchasing power. The Federal Reserve targets two to three percent annual inflation, meaning money loses half its purchasing power every twenty-five to thirty-five years. Though gradual, the cumulative effect is devastating for savers.

A dollar saved in 1970 has lost 87% of its purchasing power by 2024. What cost $100 then requires $750 today. This isn't economic growth, it's currency debasement. Your grandfather's advice to save money in a bank account made sense under the gold standard when money held its value. Today, that same advice guarantees slow-motion impoverishment.

This inflationary system forces a critical choice: invest or grow poorer. There is no standing still. Money sitting in checking accounts or stuffed in mattresses slowly dissolves like ice in the sun. Only by converting cash into productive assets can you maintain and grow purchasing power over time. This is why the wealthy hold minimal cash relative to net worth, they understand that in an inflationary system, cash quietly decays, and is useful only as a temporary medium of exchange or emergency buffer.

The money supply expansion accelerates during crises, creating massive wealth transfers to asset holders. In 2020 alone, the Federal Reserve created more dollars than existed in the first two hundred years of American history. This unprecedented monetary expansion drove asset prices to record highs while everyday goods became increasingly expensive. Those holding assets, stocks, real estate, businesses, saw their wealth explode. Those holding cash watched their purchasing power evaporate.

## The Banking System's Multiplication Effect

Fractional-reserve lending amplifies monetary effects throughout the economy in ways most people never understand. Here's how the magic trick works:

When you deposit $1,000 in a bank, they don't keep that money in a vault waiting for you to withdraw it. Under current reserve requirements, they might keep only $100 and lend out $900. The borrower deposits that $900 in their bank, which keeps $90 and lends out $810. This process continues, with each iteration creating new money:

- Your initial deposit: $1,000
- First loan created: $900
- Second loan created: $810
- Third loan created: $729
- Fourth loan created: $656
- And on and on...

Through this process, your initial $1,000 deposit creates

up to $10,000 in new money supply. This isn't fraud or trickery, it's the designed function of fractional reserve banking. Think of it like a single seed being planted, harvested, replanted, and multiplied over and over again. The system literally creates money from thin air, limited only by reserve requirements and lending demand.

Banks profit from the interest spread between what they pay depositors and charge borrowers. While your savings account pays 0.01% annually, the bank lends your money at dramatically higher rates:

- **Mortgages:** 4-7%
- **Auto loans:** 5-9%
- **Personal loans:** 8-12%
- **Credit cards:** 18-29%

This spread represents pure profit extracted from the productive economy. A bank paying you 0.5% on savings while charging 20% on credit cards earns forty times more on your money than they pay you. Understanding this system reveals why being a borrower at high rates while saving at low rates guarantees wealth transfer from you to banks.

Credit cards represent the most egregious example of this wealth extraction. While savings accounts pay less than one percent annually, credit cards charge fifteen to twenty-five percent. If you carry a $5,000 credit card balance at twenty percent interest while keeping $5,000 in savings at one percent, you're losing nineteen percent annually, $950 per year. This negative arbitrage affects millions of Americans who simultaneously save and carry high-interest debt, not understanding they're paying banks to hold their own money.

## The Power of Compound Interest

Albert Einstein allegedly called compound interest the eighth wonder of the world, saying "He who understands it, earns it; he who doesn't, pays it." Whether Einstein actually said this or not, the sentiment captures a fundamental truth about wealth building that most people never fully grasp.

Compound interest means earning returns not just on principal but on accumulated returns as well. It starts slowly, almost imperceptibly, but accelerates exponentially over time. The growth curve looks like this:

$1,000 INVESTED AT 10% annual returns:

- Year 1: Earn $100 (total: $1,100)
- Year 5: Earn $161 (total: $1,610)
- Year 10: Earn $259 (total: $2,594)
- Year 20: Earn $673 (total: $6,727)
- Year 30: Earn $1,745 (total: $17,449)
- Year 40: Earn $4,526 (total: $45,259)

Notice how the annual earnings in year forty exceed the entire initial investment by over four times? Behold the magic of compounding, your money makes money, which makes money, which makes money, creating a snowball effect that eventually becomes an avalanche.

The Rule of 72 provides a quick way to calculate doubling time for any growth rate. Simply divide 72 by the annual return percentage to get years required to double your money:

- At 6% returns: Money doubles every 12 years
- At 8% returns: Money doubles every 9 years
- At 10% returns: Money doubles every 7.2 years
- At 12% returns: Money doubles every 6 years

THIS MEANS STARTING to invest at twenty-five versus thirty-five costs you an entire doubling period, worth hundreds of thousands or millions in retirement. The mathematics are unforgiving and absolute.

The difference between starting early and starting late cannot be overstated. A 25-year-old investing $500 monthly at 10% returns will have $3.16 million by age 65. A 35-year-old investing the same amount will have only $1.13 million. The ten-year delay costs over $2 million despite investing only $60,000 less in total contributions. This mathematical reality makes every year of delay exponentially expensive.

Compound interest is like yeast in dough: invisible at first, but soon you've got a money loaf that could feed generations.

## Time Value and Velocity of Money

The time value of money principle states that money available now is worth more than the same amount in the future due to its earning capacity. This principle governs every financial decision, from taking a lump sum versus annuity to deciding whether to pay cash or finance a purchase. Every dollar spent today represents not just that dollar but all future returns it could have generated.

Consider the true cost of purchases through this lens:

- A $50,000 car purchased at age 30 doesn't just

cost $50,000, invested at 8% until age 65, it would grow to $739,567

- A $5 daily coffee habit costs $1,825 annually, which invested over 30 years becomes $223,674 (I know, I know... telling you to skip your $5 latte is the ultimate 'Boomer' financial advice. But look at the math!)
- A $100 monthly subscription over 30 years costs $36,000 but represents $226,048 in lost investment returns
- Even small purchases compound: $20 weekly on unnecessary items becomes $161,223 over 30 years

Small leaks sink great ships, and small expenses destroy great fortunes. The wealthy understand this implicitly, which is why they evaluate every expense through the lens of opportunity cost.

Money velocity matters as much as money amount. Velocity refers to how quickly money moves through investments generating returns:

- **Dead money** (checking accounts): Zero velocity, zero returns
- **Slow money** (savings accounts): Minimal velocity, sub-inflation returns
- **Active money** (index funds): High velocity, market returns
- **Leveraged money** (real estate, business): Maximum velocity, amplified returns

The wealthy understand that idle money is wasted potential. They keep money in motion, always invested, always working, always growing. Even their emergency funds often sit in high-yield accounts or money market funds, generating returns while remaining liquid. Every dollar has a job, and that job is to make more dollars.

## Cognitive Biases That Sabotage Wealth

Human brains evolved for immediate survival in small tribes on the African savanna, not for building wealth in complex modern economies. Every cognitive bias that helped our ancestors survive now sabotages financial success. Understanding these biases is the first step to overcoming them.

**Present bias** causes people to overvalue immediate rewards versus future benefits. Our ancestors needed to consume resources immediately before they spoiled or were stolen. In modern times, this manifests as spending rather than saving, choosing immediate pleasure over future security. Studies show people will choose $100 today over $150 in one year, despite the 50% return representing an exceptional investment opportunity that would require finding an investment yielding 50% annually, nearly impossible in normal markets.

**Loss aversion** makes people feel losses twice as intensely as equivalent gains. This protected ancestors from risks that could mean death, but now prevents people from taking calculated risks with positive expected returns. The stock market has returned roughly 10% annually for a century, yet people avoid investing because they fear temporary downturns more than they value long-term gains.

**Social comparison** drives lifestyle inflation as people evaluate status relatively rather than absolutely. In ancestral tribes, relative status determined mating opportunities and resource access. Today, this drives people to:

- Buy cars they can't afford to match neighbors
- Upgrade homes to keep up with friends
- Purchase designer goods for status signaling
- Take expensive vacations for social media validation

Studies show people would rather earn $50,000 when others earn $25,000 than earn $100,000 when others earn $200,000, choosing relative superiority over absolute prosperity. This preference for relative wealth over absolute wealth keeps people trapped in status games that prevent real wealth accumulation.

## Breaking Free from Psychological Traps

Mental accounting causes people to treat money differently based on arbitrary categories. Common mental accounting errors include:

- Splurging with bonuses while being frugal with salary
- Spending tax refunds frivolously while carefully saving regular income
- Treating inherited money as "found money" to waste
- Being willing to drive across town to save $10 on a $50 purchase but not to save $10 on a $1,000 purchase

All money is fungible, a dollar is a dollar regardless of its source. Yet people create elaborate mental categories that lead to irrational financial decisions. Casinos exploit this brilliantly by converting money to chips, making losses feel less real. Credit cards work similarly, disconnecting spending from payment.

The sunk cost fallacy keeps people trapped in poor financial decisions. Examples are everywhere:

- Continuing to pay for unused gym memberships because you "already paid for the year"
- Holding losing stocks because selling would "lock in the loss"
- Staying in expensive apartments because you "already paid the deposit"
- Keeping subscriptions you don't use because you "might need them someday"

This bias causes people to throw good money after bad rather than cutting losses. Every financial decision should be evaluated based on future prospects, not past investments. The money is already gone, the only question is whether continuing makes sense going forward.

Confirmation bias makes people seek information supporting existing beliefs while ignoring contradicting evidence. Investors convinced the market will crash read doom-and-gloom articles while missing the ongoing bull market. Those believing in get-rich-quick schemes find anecdotes of success while ignoring statistics showing 99% failure rates.

Breaking free from these psychological traps requires systems, not willpower:

- **Automation** prevents present bias by moving money to investments before you can spend it
- **Index fund investing** eliminates overconfidence by accepting market returns

- **Written investment policies** prevent emotional decisions during volatility
- **Spending plans** (not budgets) align spending with values rather than impulses
- **Regular financial reviews** force confrontation with reality rather than comfortable delusions

The key is recognizing that your brain isn't your ally in building wealth. Evolution optimized your psychology for surviving on the savanna, not thriving in capitalism. Design systems that succeed despite psychology, not because of it.

## Mathematical Certainty Over Hope

The modern financial system creates unprecedented opportunities for wealth building, but only for those who understand its mechanics. Never before in human history has the average person had access to such powerful wealth-building tools:

- **Global stock markets** accessible with zero commissions
- **Index funds** providing instant diversification at near-zero cost
- **Tax-advantaged accounts** sheltering gains from taxation
- **Compound interest** working 24/7/365
- **Information and education** freely available online
- **Automated investing** removing human error and emotion

The combination of fiat currency, inflation, compound

interest, and global markets means anyone can build wealth through patient investing. You don't need to pick winning stocks, time the market, or have inside information. You simply need to understand these fundamental mechanics and position yourself to benefit from them rather than be victimized by them.

The mathematics of wealth building are immutable and follow a predictable sequence:

1. **Save more than you spend** - Create investable surplus
2. **Invest the difference** - Put money to work in productive assets
3. **Let compound returns work over time** - Patience pays exponentially
4. **Protect what you build** - Insurance and diversification preserve gains
5. **Scale your income** - Accelerate the entire process through earning more

These principles worked a century ago, work today, and will work a century from now. Technology changes, markets fluctuate, economies cycle, but mathematics remains constant. While others chase the latest investment fad or get-rich-quick scheme, you can build lasting wealth on mathematical certainty.

The path forward is clear. Understanding money's true nature, as a tool that can work independently of human labor, transforms your relationship with wealth. Recognizing the modern monetary system's inflationary bias positions you to benefit rather than suffer. Grasping compound interest's exponential power motivates early and consistent investing. Acknowledging psychological biases allows you to design systems that overcome them.

Build your wealth on mathematical certainty, not hope or speculation. The formulas don't care about your background, your education, or your starting point. They simply work, multiplying money according to unchanging laws, available to anyone willing to understand and apply them. The foundation is now laid. The principles are clear. The only question remaining is whether you'll act on this knowledge or let another day, month, or year pass while your wealth-building potential slowly erodes to inflation and inaction.

## Chapter 1 Quick Wins:

Calculate Your True Hourly Wage - Divide your annual after-tax income by total hours spent on work (including commute, preparation, recovery). Use this number to evaluate all purchases: "Is this worth X hours of my life?"

**2**

———

# THE DEBT FREEDOM FOUNDATION

Sarah and Emma, identical twins, started their careers at the same accounting firm with identical $45,000 salaries. At their 25th birthday dinner, they laughed about how they even drove the same Honda Civic model, just different colors. That's where their financial paths diverged.

Sarah believed in "using credit wisely to build her life." She financed a new car, $35,000 at 6% because "reliable transportation is an investment." She furnished her apartment beautifully on credit cards, accumulating $8,000 in balances. "I deserve to live well after college," she reasoned. When her company offered tuition reimbursement up to $10,000 annually, she enrolled in an MBA program costing $60,000 total, borrowing the difference. "It's good debt," her banker assured her.

Her monthly payments:
- Car: $580
- Credit cards (minimums): $240
- Student loans: $550
- New furniture loan: $150

• Updated wardrobe for her "professional image": $280 on a store card

Total: $1,800 monthly in debt service.

Emma took a different path. She bought a five-year-old Toyota for $5,000 cash after saving for six months. She furnished her apartment from Facebook Marketplace and estate sales, same quality, 80% less cost. She took free online courses from MIT and Stanford, earned Google certifications, and let her company pay for targeted training. "Why pay for knowledge that's free?" she wondered.

Instead of debt payments, Emma invested $1,800 monthly in index funds. Some months were tough, her car needed repairs, her apartment wasn't Instagram-perfect, and she watched Sarah get promoted faster initially thanks to that MBA.

By age 30, Sarah was earning $75,000 (the MBA helped) but still had $87,000 in debt. Emma earned $65,000 but had $147,000 invested. Sarah justified the gap: "My earning potential is higher."

By age 35, their salaries had converged, both earning around $85,000. Sarah's MBA advantage had plateaued. She was still making payments. Emma's investments had grown to $412,000.

At 40, Sarah made her final debt payment. She'd paid $147,000 total to eliminate $103,000 in original balances. She celebrated with dinner at the restaurant where she and Emma had celebrated their 25th birthday. "Finally free to start building wealth," she posted on social media.

Emma commented with a heart emoji. She didn't mention her portfolio had just crossed $892,000.

The reunion was revealing. Sarah confessed, "I spent fifteen years working for banks instead of myself. Every raise went to payments. Every bonus disappeared into interest. I was running on a treadmills lots of motion, no progress."

Today, Sarah teaches financial literacy at the community center. Her opening slide shows two numbers:

- $147,000: What she paid to learn her lesson
- $892,000: What the lesson cost her

"The difference between my sister and me wasn't income, intelligence, or luck," she tells every class. "It was understanding that debt makes you poorer while appearing richer, and investing makes you richer while appearing poorer. By the time appearances matched reality, the game was already over."


## The Mathematics of Debt Destruction

Debt behaves like treacle around your ankles. You can still move at first, but each step costs more energy, more time, and more money, until forward progress feels impossible. Every dollar paid in interest is a dollar that could have been invested for compound growth. The average American household pays over $8,000 annually in interest. That money doesn't build security, freedom, or options, it simply disappears. And when you factor in what those dollars *could* have become if invested, the true cost of debt multiplies far beyond the statement balance. Over thirty years, this represents $240,000 in direct payments plus $2.7 million in lost compound growth opportunity when you factor in what that money could have earned in the market.

Think about that for a moment. Not only are you paying a quarter million dollars to banks, but you're also missing out on nearly three million in wealth you could have built. This is the devastating double punch of debt, the money you pay and the money you never make.

The mathematics of debt works against you with the same relentless power that investment mathematics works for you, but in reverse. Take a typical $10,000 credit card balance at 20% interest. Making only minimum payments of 2% of the balance, you'll spend 26 years paying it off. The total cost? $31,000 for that original $10,000 borrowed, a 210% premium for the privilege of spending money you didn't have.

But here's where it gets truly painful. That same $31,000, if invested over those 26 years at market returns, would grow to approximately $334,000. The true cost of that credit card debt isn't the $21,000 in interest, it's the $334,000 in wealth you'll never build. That's a 3,240% opportunity cost that transforms potential millionaires into perpetual debtors.

High-interest debt creates a vicious cycle that becomes increasingly difficult to escape:

- Interest charges reduce your available cash flow
- Less cash flow means you can't save for emergencies
- No emergency fund forces you to borrow when surprises hit
- More borrowing means higher interest payments
- Higher payments further reduce cash flow
- The spiral continues, gaining momentum like a snowball rolling downhill

Breaking this cycle requires understanding both the mathematical and psychological components of debt, then applying systematic strategies to reverse the momentum. Every dollar servicing debt has negative velocity, it leaves your control and generates returns for lenders instead of you. Meanwhile, a dollar invested has positive velocity, generating returns that generate more returns. This difference creates an exponentially growing wealth gap between debtors and investors.

Two people earning identical incomes can end up with vastly different wealth simply based on whether their dollars flow toward debt service or investment growth. One retires wealthy, the other retires worried. The difference? How they handled debt in their thirties and forties.

## The Debt Avalanche Method

The debt avalanche method provides the mathematically optimal path to debt freedom by minimizing total interest paid. Here's how it works:

1. List all debts from highest to lowest interest rate (ignore balances completely)
2. Make minimum payments on everything to protect your credit
3. Attack the highest rate debt with every available dollar beyond minimums
4. Once eliminated, apply its entire payment to the next highest rate
5. Continue until debt-free

Let's look at a typical American debt portfolio:

- **Credit Card A:** 24% interest, $5,000 balance, $150 minimum payment
- **Credit Card B:** 18% interest, $3,000 balance, $90 minimum payment
- **Auto Loan:** 6% interest, $15,000 balance, $350 minimum payment

- **Student Loan:** 4% interest, $25,000 balance, $250 minimum payment

Total debt: $48,000 with $840 in minimum payments.

The avalanche method says attack Credit Card A first, regardless of its balance being smaller than the auto loan or student loan. Why? Because every dollar eliminating 24% interest is equivalent to earning a guaranteed 24% return, better than any investment available to retail investors.

When you run the numbers, the results are compelling. Using the avalanche method with $2,000 monthly payments, you'll be debt-free in 28 months and pay $5,832 in total interest. Paying debts randomly might take 35 months and cost over $9,000 in interest. The avalanche saves you $3,168 and seven months of payments. That saved $3,168, invested over twenty years, becomes $34,000, showing how optimal debt elimination strategies create massive long-term wealth differences.

Advanced avalanche strategies involve regularly reordering your debt priority list:

- Variable rate debts can see rate increases, moving them higher in priority
- Balance transfer offers can temporarily reduce rates, moving debts lower
- Home equity line rates fluctuate with prime rate changes
- Monthly reevaluation ensures you're always attacking the highest rate debt

The avalanche method also clarifies investment decisions when you're carrying debt. Any investment return below your highest debt interest rate is mathematically inferior to debt payment. Contributing to a 401(k) with 6% expected returns while carrying 18% credit card debt means accepting a guaranteed 12% loss. The only exception? Employer matching, which provides immediate 50-100% returns that exceed even high-interest debt rates.

## The Debt Snowball Psychology

Mathematically, the avalanche method is optimal. But behaviorally, the snowball method is often more effective because it accounts for human psychology, and psychology often determines whether you succeed or fail. Here's the snowball approach:

1. List debts from smallest to largest balance (completely ignore interest rates)
2. Make minimum payments on everything
3. Attack the smallest debt first with all extra money
4. Celebrate when you eliminate it
5. Roll that payment to the next smallest debt

The quick win from eliminating your smallest debt provides psychological momentum that sustains motivation through the longer journey toward complete debt freedom. It sounds irrational, but behavioral economists have proven it works.

Studies show people using the snowball method are more likely to complete their debt elimination journey, despite paying more interest. Why? Because the psychological boost from early wins outweighs the mathematical disadvantage. For someone with five debts, eliminating one quickly makes the remaining four feel manageable. This perceived progress matters more than optimal mathematics if it's the difference between success and giving up.

The snowball method leverages powerful psychological principles:

- **The Zeigarnik Effect:** Uncompleted tasks occupy mental bandwidth, each debt you eliminate frees cognitive resources
- **Goal Gradient Effect:** We naturally accelerate effort as we approach completion, fewer debts remaining increases motivation
- **Dopamine Response:** Small wins trigger reward chemicals, creating addiction to debt elimination progress
- **Momentum Building:** Early success builds confidence for tackling larger challenges

The ideal approach might be a hybrid strategy. Start with the snowball method to build momentum and establish the debt elimination habit. After eliminating one or two small debts and building confidence, switch to the avalanche method to minimize interest. This combines psychology initially with mathematics ultimately.

Some people alternate between methods, using snowball when motivation wanes and avalanche when discipline is strong. There's no shame in adapting your strategy to your emotional state. The only shame is in not addressing debt at all.

## The Hidden Costs of "Good Debt"

Society promotes certain debts as "good" mortgages build equity, student loans are investments in yourself, business debt creates growth. Financial advisors, real estate agents, and educational institutions perpetuate these myths because their businesses depend on your debt acceptance. While these debts can theoretically be tools for building wealth, they're often wealth destroyers wearing investment costumes.

Student loans exemplify this dangerous misconception. The average graduate carries $37,000 in student debt at 5-7% interest. Monthly payments of $400 for ten years total $48,000. But here's what nobody calculates, the opportunity cost. That $400 monthly invested for forty years until retirement becomes $2.5 million at historical market returns.

Many degrees don't generate enough additional income to justify this massive opportunity cost:

- A degree costing $100,000 that increases income by $10,000 annually might seem worthwhile
- But after taxes, that's only $7,000 in additional take-home pay
- Loan payments eat $1,000 monthly ($12,000 annually)
- You're actually going backward, not even considering opportunity cost

The student loan crisis extends beyond individual impact. Graduates delay homeownership, entrepreneurship, and family formation due to debt burden. Meanwhile, universities increase tuition at triple the inflation rate, knowing student loans enable payment. This creates an unsustainable bubble, inflated prices supported by crushing debt.

Mortgages, while enabling homeownership, can destroy wealth through over-leveraging and true cost ignorance. A

$400,000 mortgage at 7% over thirty years costs $958,000 total...$558,000 in interest alone. But that's just the beginning:

- Property taxes: $180,000 over thirty years
- Insurance: $60,000
- Maintenance (1-2% annually): $150,000
- HOA fees: $90,000
- True total cost: Over $1.4 million

The house that supposedly builds wealth might actually prevent it through excessive debt service and associated costs. Many people would build more wealth renting cheaply and investing the difference.

Business debt receives similar "good debt" treatment but often destroys entrepreneurs. Small businesses fail at 80% rates within five years, leaving owners with personal guarantees on business debt. Even successful businesses can become debt slaves, with owners working primarily to service loans rather than build equity. The leverage that supposedly accelerates growth often accelerates failure when revenue fluctuates.

## The Velocity of Debt Elimination

Debt elimination velocity determines how quickly you achieve freedom and begin building wealth. Small increases in payment amounts create dramatic timeline compression. Here's what acceleration looks like:

- Extra $100 monthly on a $200,000 mortgage saves $68,000 in interest and eliminates the loan six years early

- That's a 680% return on the extra payment investment
- Extra $500 monthly might eliminate debt three years earlier
- Those three years of payments, redirected to investments, could become $500,000 by retirement

Every month shaved off debt payments is a month added to wealth accumulation, with compound interest working for rather than against you.

Accelerating debt elimination requires finding or creating additional cash flow:

**Income increases:**

- Work overtime or take extra shifts
- Start a side hustle (even 10 hours weekly can add $500-1,000 monthly)
- Negotiate raises or change jobs
- Sell services you already know (tutoring, consulting, freelancing)
- Drive for ride-sharing or food delivery

**Expense reductions:**

- Sell unused items (average household has $3,000+ in sellable clutter)
- Eliminate subscriptions (average American has 11 costing $273 monthly)
- Downgrade services temporarily
- Cook at home instead of eating out
- Find free entertainment alternatives

**Windfall opportunities:**

- Tax refunds (averaging $3,000)
- Bonuses
- Inheritances
- Gifts
- Settlement payments
- Garage sale proceeds
- Rebates and cash-back rewards

Most people criminally waste windfalls on consumption or lifestyle inflation. Instead, applying them to debt creates permanent benefit. A $5,000 tax refund eliminating credit card debt saves $1,000+ annually in interest, a 20% permanent return. That $1,000 annual savings, invested over twenty years, becomes $57,000.

## Strategic Debt Restructuring

Debt restructuring can accelerate elimination without requiring additional payments. Its financial engineering to reduce interest costs while maintaining payment levels.

**Balance Transfer Strategy:**

Balance transfer cards offering 0% introductory rates provide breathing room to attack principal without interest accumulation. Transferring $10,000 from 20% to 0% for eighteen months saves $3,000 in interest, effectively creating $3,000 for debt elimination.

Success requires careful planning:

- Transfer fees typically run 3-5%, so ensure savings exceed costs
- Track promotional period end dates religiously

- Never make new purchases on balance transfer cards
- Payments apply to lowest-rate balances first
- Chain multiple transfers to maintain 0% rates throughout elimination

**Debt Consolidation Loans:**

Consolidating multiple high-interest debts into single lower-rate loans reduces both payment complexity and interest costs. Three credit cards averaging 22% consolidated into a 12% personal loan cuts interest costs nearly in half.

Warning signs to avoid:

- Never consolidate then rack up new credit card balances
- Close consolidated accounts or freeze cards to prevent reuse
- Don't extend payment terms just to lower monthly amounts
- Avoid consolidation loans with prepayment penalties

**Home Equity Danger:**

Home equity loans can eliminate high-interest debt but carry serious risks. Converting 20% credit card debt to 7% home equity debt reduces interest by 65%. However, you're converting unsecured debt to secured debt backed by your home, if you can't pay credit cards, you damage your credit; if you can't pay home equity loans, you lose your house.

## The Zero-Based Budget Revolution

Zero-based budgeting transforms debt elimination from hopeful intention to mathematical certainty. Every dollar of income receives a specific assignment before the month begins. Income minus expenses equals exactly zero, with surplus automatically attacking debt.

Traditional budgeting fails because it's reactive, tracking where money went rather than directing where it goes. Zero-based budgeting is proactive, making spending decisions intentionally rather than impulsively.

Creating your zero-based budget:

1. List all income sources for the month
2. List all fixed expenses (rent, utilities, insurance)
3. Allocate funds to variable necessities (food, gas, clothing)
4. Assign money to debt payments above minimums
5. Designate any remaining to strategic savings
6. Total must equal exactly zero

Most people discover $500-1,000 monthly in unconscious spending that can be redirected to debt elimination. The goal isn't deprivation but intentionality, ensuring money goes to priorities rather than evaporating mysteriously.

THE ENVELOPE SYSTEM:

Physical cash in labeled envelopes enforces zero-based budgets for variable spending:

- Withdraw allocated cash for groceries, entertainment, discretionary spending
- Place in labeled envelopes
- When empty, spending stops until next month
- Spent cash creates psychological pain that cards avoid

This tangible system makes abstract budgets concrete, preventing overspending that digital transactions enable.

## Breaking the Paycheck-to-Paycheck Prison

Seventy-eight percent of Americans live paycheck-to-paycheck, including many six-figure earners. This isn't about income level, it's about the relationship between income and expenses. Breaking free requires creating a buffer.

**The $1,000 Starting Point:**

Start by creating a micro-emergency fund of $1,000 while making only minimum debt payments. This violates avalanche mathematics but provides essential psychological security. This buffer prevents new debt from minor emergencies:

- Car repairs
- Medical bills
- Home maintenance
- Appliance replacement

Once established, resume aggressive debt elimination knowing surprises won't derail progress.

The paycheck-to-paycheck cycle creates problems beyond money:

- Financial stress reduces IQ by 13 points
- Chronic stress causes health problems
- Relationships suffer from money arguments
- Work performance decreases from distraction
- Poor decisions perpetuate the cycle

Creating margin requires attacking from both sides simultaneously. Even a 10% improvement on both, 10% more income, 10% less expenses, creates 20% margin for debt elimination. This margin compounds as eliminated debt payments become additional margin.

## The Debt-Free Lifestyle Architecture

Living debt-free requires fundamentally different thinking than what society considers normal. It means:

- Buying cars with cash
- Avoiding credit card balances entirely
- Saving for purchases rather than financing
- Delaying gratification until you can afford things
- Saying no to lifestyle inflation

Without debt payments, income stretches dramatically further. The average household pays $1,500+ monthly in non-mortgage debt. Eliminating these payments equals an $18,000 annual after-tax raise. This freed cash flow, redirected to investments, accelerates wealth building exponentially.

Debt-free living changes purchase psychology through forced patience. When you must save for purchases, you evaluate whether you really want them. The cooling-off period often eliminates desire. Items you still want after saving are purchased intentionally, increasing satisfaction while decreasing consumption.

The benefits extend far beyond money:

**Personal benefits:**

- Better sleep without payment worries
- Reduced anxiety and stress
- Improved physical health
- Greater life satisfaction
- Freedom to pursue passions

**Relationship benefits:**

- Fewer money arguments
- Aligned financial goals
- Ability to be generous
- Shared accomplishment
- Modeling good habits for children

**Career benefits:**

- Job choices based on fulfillment, not just salary
- Ability to take calculated risks
- Entrepreneurial opportunities
- Negotiating from strength, not desperation
- Early retirement possibility

The debt-free lifestyle enables the life you actually want rather than the one debt demands. It's not about restriction, it's about freedom. Freedom from payments, freedom from worry, freedom to pursue opportunities, freedom to help others, freedom to live intentionally rather than reactively.

Your journey to debt freedom starts with a decision, the decision that you've paid banks enough, that you deserve to keep what you earn, that your future self deserves better than perpetual payments. The strategies are proven and the math is certain; the only variable is your commitment to change. Once debt is no longer draining your cash flow, the next question becomes obvious: where should your money go next?

## Chapter 2 Quick Wins:

Cancel Three Subscriptions - Identify your three least-used subscriptions and cancel them.

3

***

# HIGH-PERFORMANCE
# SAVINGS AND BANKING

Savings form the foundation upon which all wealth is built. Without savings, you cannot invest. Without investments, you cannot build wealth. Without wealth, you remain enslaved to employment forever. Yet most Americans save nothing, with 60% unable to cover a $1,000 emergency and 78% living paycheck to paycheck. This isn't primarily an income problem, it's a systems problem. Households earning over $100,000 annually often have less savings than those earning $50,000 with proper systems.

The strategic savings hierarchy optimizes where each dollar goes for maximum benefit:

- **First Priority:** A starter emergency fund of $1,000-2,500, preventing debt accumulation from minor crises. This small buffer prevents the negative compound interest spiral where car repairs become credit card debt and eventually turn into decades of payments.

- **Second Priority:** Employer 401k match, free
  money with guaranteed 50-100% returns that no
  other investment can match.
- **Third Priority:** High-interest debt elimination,
  providing guaranteed returns equal to interest
  rates. Paying off 24% credit cards is equivalent to
  earning 24% guaranteed returns.
- **Fourth Priority:** A full 3-6 month emergency
  fund protecting against job loss or major crises.
- **Fifth Priority:** Retirement account maximization
  for tax-advantaged growth. Only after these
  foundations should you consider taxable
  investments or aggressive strategies.

This hierarchy isn't arbitrary but mathematically optimized based on risk-adjusted returns. Each level provides either risk reduction or return enhancement that justifies its priority. Skipping levels to chase exciting investments while neglecting foundations is like building a penthouse on quicksand. The structure will eventually collapse, destroying everything built above weak foundations. Consider someone investing in cryptocurrency while carrying credit card debt, they're accepting volatile potential returns while paying guaranteed 20%+ losses to credit card companies.

THE PSYCHOLOGICAL BENEFITS of following the hierarchy compound the mathematical advantages. Each completed level provides security and confidence that enables taking appropriate risks at higher levels. Someone with six months of expenses saved can weather market volatility that would panic someone with no buffer. This emotional stability prevents costly panic selling and enables long-term thinking essential for wealth building.

The flexibility within the hierarchy allows customization for individual situations while maintaining optimization principles:

- High-income earners might build larger emergency funds given bigger monthly obligations
- Those with variable income need bigger buffers than stable salary earners
- Single-income families require more protection than dual-income households
- The hierarchy provides framework while allowing personal calibration

## The Coffee Shop Experiment

A local coffee shop owner decided to run an experiment with two tip jars.

The first jar sat by the register with a sign: "Tips Appreciated!" Customers dropped in change when they remembered, felt generous, or had coins to discard. Monthly total: $47.

The second jar was different. The owner installed a tablet suggesting tip amounts, $1, $2, $3, automatically appearing after each card payment. One tap, done. No thinking required. Monthly total: $1,247.

Same customers. Same service. Same coffee. Twenty-six times more money.

The owner realized this wasn't about coffee or even tips, it was about human nature. When action requires decision, it rarely happens. When action happens automatically, it always happens.

She took the lesson home. Instead of "trying to save

more," she split her direct deposit: 20% to savings before the rest hit checking. Instead of "investing when she had extra," she scheduled weekly transfers to her investment account. Instead of "shopping for better rates when she had time," she opened a high-yield account that afternoon.

A year later, she'd saved $12,000, more than the previous five years combined. Her income hadn't changed. Her systems had.

The coffee shop still has both tip jars. She keeps them as a daily reminder: success isn't about willpower or windfalls. It's about systems that make the right thing the easy thing.

## The Psychology of Automated Wealth

Automation is the secret weapon of wealth builders, turning good intentions into guaranteed execution. When savings happen automatically, they actually happen. When savings require manual action, they rarely happen. The difference between financial success and failure often comes down to setting up automatic transfers that run without thought or willpower. It's like having a tiny robot accountant who never sleeps, never complains, and always shows up on payday. Studies show automatic savers accumulate 5-10 times more than manual savers with identical incomes and intentions.

Configure your direct deposit to split paychecks automatically before money reaches your spending account. Send 20% to savings before the remainder hits checking. What you don't see, you don't miss. This "pay yourself first" principle ensures savings happen regardless of month-to-month discipline fluctuations. After a few months, you'll adapt to living on the reduced amount while wealth accumulates invisibly in the background. The psychological principle of hedonic adaptation means happiness levels return to baseline despite income changes, use this to your advantage.

Escalating automation amplifies results over time through imperceptible lifestyle adjustments:

- Start with 10% automatic savings if 20% seems impossible
- Increase by 1% quarterly, unnoticeable lifestyle changes that compound into dramatic wealth accumulation
- Someone earning $50,000 saving 10% initially and increasing 1% quarterly reaches 25% savings rate in under four years while barely noticing the lifestyle adjustment
- After five years, they're saving $15,000 annually versus $5,000 initially, tripling wealth accumulation through gradual automation increases

Multiple automation streams create comprehensive wealth building systems:

- Automate 401k contributions through payroll deduction
- Schedule weekly transfers to high-yield savings
- Set up monthly transfers to investment accounts
- Configure quarterly transfers to opportunity funds
- Each automation removes a decision point where discipline might fail
- The cumulative effect transforms ordinary earners into automatic wealth builders without daily willpower requirements

The automation timing strategy optimizes cash flow while ensuring savings priority. Schedule transfers for the day after paycheck deposits, guaranteeing money moves before spending temptations arise. Align bill payments after savings transfers, ensuring wealth building takes precedence. Use separate accounts for different purposes, bills, savings, investments, with automatic routing to each. This systematic approach makes proper money management effortless rather than exhausting.

## High-Yield Savings Account Optimization

The difference between traditional savings accounts paying 0.01% and high-yield accounts paying 4-5% represents a 400-500x interest differential. On a $10,000 emergency fund, that's the difference between earning $1 or $500 annually. Yet most people keep savings in checking accounts or traditional savings, literally leaving hundreds or thousands on the table annually. Over a decade, this seemingly small optimization can mean $5,000 or more in lost earnings, enough to fund a Roth IRA for an entire year.

Online banks offer the highest yields because they lack expensive branch networks and legacy technology infrastructure:

- Marcus by Goldman Sachs, Ally, American Express Personal Savings, and Capital One 360 consistently offer top rates
- These accounts are FDIC insured to $250,000, providing identical safety to traditional banks with dramatically superior returns
- The only difference is where profits go, to

shareholders in traditional banks or to depositors in high-yield accounts

Opening high-yield accounts takes minutes online and provides immediate benefit regardless of balance size. Link to existing checking for easy transfers, most support same-day or next-day transfers. Some offer ATM access for true emergency needs. The supposed inconvenience that keeps people in low-yield accounts is largely imaginary, you can access high-yield savings as quickly as traditional accounts while earning 500 times more interest.

Account churning strategies maximize promotional rates offered to new customers:

- Banks frequently offer bonuses for opening accounts and maintaining balances
- A $10,000 deposit might earn a $200-500 bonus plus ongoing interest
- Monitor sites like Doctor of Credit for the latest offers
- Opening 2-3 new accounts annually for bonuses can generate $1,000+ in additional returns beyond interest
- The minimal effort of account applications pays better hourly rates than most jobs

The relationship between Federal Reserve rates and savings yields creates timing opportunities. When Fed rates rise, online banks increase rates quickly while traditional banks lag. Move money immediately when rates rise. Conversely, when rates fall, some banks maintain higher rates temporarily to retain deposits. Having multiple high-yield accounts allows shifting to whoever offers the best rates at any moment.

## Money Market Funds and Treasury Strategies

Money market funds provide slightly higher yields than savings accounts with comparable safety for sophisticated savers. These funds invest in short-term government securities, commercial paper, and certificates of deposit. Yields track Federal Reserve rates closely, currently offering 5-5.5% returns. While not FDIC insured, government money market funds have never lost money for retail investors and provide excellent savings alternatives for those willing to accept minimal additional complexity.

The distinction between different money market fund types affects both risk and returns:

- **Government money market funds:** Invest exclusively in U.S. government securities, providing maximum safety with slightly lower yields
- **Prime money market funds:** Include corporate debt, offering marginally higher yields with slightly more risk
- **Tax-exempt money market funds:** Invest in municipal securities, providing tax-free income valuable for high earners
- Choose based on your tax bracket and risk tolerance

Treasury ladders optimize yields while maintaining liquidity through strategic maturity management. Buy Treasury bills maturing every month for three to six months out.

As each matures, reinvest at current rates while maintaining monthly liquidity. This strategy captures higher yields than savings accounts while keeping money accessible. With TreasuryDirect, you can build ladders with as little as $100 per rung, making this institutional strategy accessible to regular investors.

The mechanics of building Treasury ladders deserve detailed understanding:

- Start by dividing your savings beyond immediate needs into 4-6 equal portions
- Purchase 4-week, 8-week, 13-week, 17-week, 26-week, and 52-week Treasury bills with each portion
- As the 4-week bill matures, roll it into a new 52-week bill
- This creates a ladder with bills maturing regularly while earning longer-term rates
- During rising rate environments, shorten maturities to capture increasing yields
- During falling rate environments, extend maturities to lock in higher rates

Bonds provide inflation protection for long-term savings, offering unique advantages unavailable elsewhere. These government bonds pay base rates plus inflation adjustments, protecting purchasing power automatically. Current composite rates exceed 5%, far surpassing traditional savings. The $10,000 annual purchase limit per person ($20,000 for couples) and one-year lockup period make them unsuitable for emergency funds but excellent for medium-term savings goals. The often-overlooked additional $5,000 purchase option through tax refunds effectively raises limits to $15,000 per person annually.

## Certificates of Deposit Strategy

CDs offer guaranteed returns for committed timeframes, providing certainty in uncertain markets. While less liquid than savings accounts, they provide higher yields for money you won't need immediately. A well-constructed CD ladder provides both higher yields and maintained liquidity through staggered maturities, combining the best of both worlds, higher returns with regular access to portions of your money.

Build sophisticated CD ladders by dividing savings into equal portions with different maturity dates:

- Split $12,000 into twelve $1,000 CDs maturing monthly
- As each matures, reinvest in a new twelve-month CD if not needed
- After one year, you have money maturing monthly while earning twelve-month rates
- This provides liquidity flexibility with enhanced returns
- More aggressive ladders might use 18 or 24-month CDs for even higher yields, accepting less frequent access for better returns

No-penalty CDs offer withdrawal flexibility while providing higher rates than regular savings, representing an often-overlooked optimization opportunity. These special CDs allow early withdrawal without sacrificing earned interest, eliminating the primary CD disadvantage. While rates are slightly lower than traditional CDs, the flexibility makes them attractive for emergency funds that need higher yields without lockup risk. Ally Bank's 11-month no-penalty CD often provides rates exceeding standard savings by 0.5-1% with complete flexibility after the first six days.

Bump-up CDs protect against rising rate environments while locking in current yields:

- These CDs allow one or two rate increases during the term if bank rates rise
- While starting rates are slightly lower than standard CDs, the option value during rising rate cycles can be substantial
- A 2-year bump-up CD started at 4% with two bump opportunities could capture 5% and 6% rates as they rise
- This significantly outperforms standard CDs locked at 4.25%

Brokered CDs purchased through investment accounts often provide superior rates and flexibility compared to bank CDs. Brokerages aggregate CDs from hundreds of banks, offering the best available rates. These CDs can be sold on secondary markets if liquidity needs arise, though prices fluctuate with interest rates. FDIC insurance still applies up to $250,000 per issuing bank, allowing millions in insured CDs across multiple banks through a single brokerage account.

## Banking Relationship Optimization

Most people bank where their parents banked or wherever seemed convenient, rarely questioning whether those relationships still serve them. This inertia costs thousands annually in fees, lost interest, and missed opportunities. Strategic banking relationships can save thousands annually through reduced fees, better rates, and enhanced services. The key is understanding what different institutions offer and structuring relationships for maximum advantage while maintaining convenience.

Credit unions often provide superior rates and lower fees than traditional banks due to their cooperative structure:

- As member-owned institutions, they return profits to members through better rates rather than enriching shareholders
- Many credit unions offer checking accounts paying 2-3% on balances up to $10,000-25,000, dramatically exceeding traditional checking
- Membership requirements are often minimal, with many open to anyone living or working in broad geographic areas
- Some allow membership through small donations to affiliated charities, effectively making them available to everyone

Online banks eliminate physical overhead, passing savings to customers through higher rates and eliminating fees. They typically offer fee-free checking, unlimited ATM reimbursements worldwide, and superior savings rates. The lack of branches concerns some, but with mobile deposit and ATM partnerships, online banks often provide better access than traditional banks with limited branch networks. Most online banks participate in shared ATM networks with 50,000+ locations, exceeding single bank branch networks.

The multi-bank strategy optimizes each relationship for specific purposes:

- Use credit unions for high-yield checking on operational funds
- Employ online banks for high-yield savings and emergency funds
- Maintain traditional bank relationships for services requiring physical presence like cashier's checks or safe deposit boxes
- Leverage investment firms for brokerage and integrated banking
- This diversification maximizes benefits while maintaining comprehensive service access

International banking provides additional optimization opportunities for sophisticated savers. Multi-currency accounts hedge against dollar weakness. Foreign banks sometimes offer higher interest rates, though currency risk must be considered. Some international accounts provide access to investments unavailable to U.S. residents. While reporting requirements exist, properly structured international accounts remain completely legal and can provide valuable diversification.

## Advanced Checking Account Strategies

Checking accounts should be optimized for transaction efficiency and rewards rather than balance holding. Keep only enough for monthly expenses plus a small buffer. Everything else should earn higher returns elsewhere. Many people keep tens of thousands in checking earning nothing when that money could generate hundreds or thousands annually in high-yield accounts. The opportunity cost of excessive checking balances compounds into massive wealth destruction over time.

Rewards checking accounts offer cash back or high interest rates for meeting monthly requirements:

- Typical requirements include ten debit transactions, direct deposit, and online banking enrollment, activities many people do anyway
- Meeting these requirements can yield 2-4% on balances up to specified limits
- For active accounts, these provide excellent returns on operational cash
- Some accounts offer 3% on $15,000 and 4% on $10,000, generating $750 annual returns on money needed for monthly expenses anyway

Multiple checking accounts can optimize for different purposes while maintaining organization:

- A bills account receives income and pays fixed expenses automatically
- A spending account holds discretionary funds with debit card access
- A business account separates side hustle finances
- A savings buffer account holds next month's expenses
- This segregation simplifies budgeting and prevents overspending while maximizing rewards and rates for each purpose

- The psychological benefit of segregation often exceeds the mathematical advantage

Checking account churning for bonuses generates substantial returns for minimal effort. Banks offer $200-600 bonuses for opening checking accounts and meeting requirements. These requirements typically include direct deposit and maintaining minimum balances for 60-90 days. Opening 4-6 checking accounts annually can generate $2,000+ in bonuses, a fantastic hourly return for application time. Track requirements carefully and close accounts after bonus periods to avoid fees.

## Business Banking Benefits

Opening business bank accounts provides benefits beyond organization, creating opportunities unavailable through personal banking alone. Business accounts access higher yields, better services, and valuable credit building opportunities. You don't need formal business registration, sole proprietorships using your Social Security number qualify for business banking. Even minimal side income justifies business banking for the advantages provided.

Business savings and money market accounts often offer higher rates than personal accounts. Business checking provides transaction capabilities personal accounts lack:

- Accepting credit cards
- Writing numerous checks
- Making frequent deposits
- Business credit cards offer superior rewards and help build business credit separate from personal credit

- This separation protects personal credit while building business borrowing capacity that could fund future ventures or real estate investments

The business credit building opportunity alone justifies opening business accounts:

- Business credit reports (Dun & Bradstreet, Experian Business, Equifax Business) are separate from personal reports
- Building strong business credit enables borrowing without personal guarantees, protecting personal assets
- Start with secured business credit cards, graduate to unsecured cards, then to lines of credit and term loans
- This parallel credit track doubles borrowing capacity

Even small side hustles benefit from business banking infrastructure. Separated finances simplify tax preparation and legitimate business deductions. Professional banking relationships can lead to business loans or lines of credit as ventures grow. The minimal effort of establishing business banking creates options and opportunities unavailable through personal accounts alone. Many successful businesses started as side hustles with proper banking infrastructure already in place.

## Chapter 3 Quick Wins:

Research Account Bonuses - Find three checking or savings accounts offering bonuses for new customers. Calculate the requirements and returns. Apply for the most profitable one this week.

4

---

# SIDE HUSTLE WEALTH
# ACCELERATION

The average millionaire has seven income streams. Not seven jobs, but seven sources generating money with varying levels of involvement. Side hustles aren't just about extra cash, they're about building skills, creating assets, and developing entrepreneurial muscles that transform your financial trajectory.

## The Reality Check Nobody Gives You:

• Time Investment: 10-20 hours weekly for 3-6 months before meaningful income

• Initial Income: $0-500 monthly (months 1-3), $500-2,000 (months 4-6), exponential growth after

• Failure Rate: 80% quit before month six, not because it doesn't work, but because they expected overnight success

• Tax Reality: Set aside 25-30% immediately

• Market Saturation: Every hustle seems saturated until you find your unique angle

Start with skills you already possess. The expertise you take for granted is worth thousands to those who lack it.

## The Excel Wizard's Awakening

Sarah had been the office Excel expert for eight years. Coworkers lined up at her desk with spreadsheet disasters, broken formulas, corrupted pivot tables, databases that wouldn't talk to each other. She'd fix them in minutes, often rebuilding their entire systems while explaining what went wrong.

"You should charge for this," they'd joke.

"Yeah, right," she'd laugh back, returning to her $52,000 salary as an inventory analyst.

One Friday, her cousin called in desperation. His startup needed financial models for investor meetings on Monday. The consultants wanted $15,000 and three weeks. Sarah built it over the weekend for free, teaching him how to update it himself.

"This would have cost us fifteen grand," he said, stunned.

Something clicked. That Sunday night, she posted in a small business Facebook group: "I'll fix your Excel nightmare for $100."

Three messages by morning.

She fixed a restaurant owner's inventory tracking system during lunch break, $100 for 45 minutes of work. She automated a realtor's commission calculations that evening, another $100 for an hour. By Friday, she'd earned $500 fixing problems that seemed impossible to others but were routine to her.

Month two, she raised prices to $200. Nobody blinked.

Month three, she created an Excel template for restaurant inventory that she'd now built three times. Posted it online for $47. Sold eight copies the first week, $376 for zero additional work.

Month six, she was earning $3,000 monthly. Her side hustle income approached her day job salary.

Month twelve, she had thirty template products selling automatically, four regular consulting clients at $500 per project, and a waiting list for custom work at $300/hour. Monthly side income: $8,000.

Her coworkers still joke about her charging for Excel help.

She doesn't mention she made $96,000 last year doing exactly that, almost double her day job salary, working fifteen hours a week on problems she could solve in her sleep.

The expertise had always been there. The only thing that changed was recognizing its value and having the courage to charge for it.

## High-Profit Side Hustles to Consider:

**Service-Based (Fast cash flow):**

- Freelance Writing: $50-500 per article, specialized writers earn $1,000+
- Virtual Assistance: $25-75/hour, specialized VAs earn $100+/hour
- Social Media Management: $500-5,000/month per client

**Digital Products (Build once, sell forever):**

- Online Courses: $10,000-1,000,000+ annually for specialized knowledge
- Templates & Tools: Create 10 templates selling 20 copies monthly at $47 = $9,400/month passive income

**E-Commerce:**

- Print-on-Demand: $10,000+/month with 30-40% margins, zero inventory risk

- Amazon FBA: Six to seven figures annually (requires $3,000-5,000 starting capital)

**Content Creation:**

- YouTube: 100,000 subscribers = $2,000-10,000/month ads + $5,000-20,000 sponsorships
- Newsletters: 1,000 paid subscribers at $5-10/month = $5,000-10,000 monthly recurring revenue

**Consulting & Real Estate:**

- Business Consulting: $150-500/hour (vs. $50/hour as employee)
- Airbnb Arbitrage: $700/month per property with 60% occupancy
- Real Estate Bird-Dogging: $500-5,000 per successful referral

The side hustle landscape has fundamentally changed. What once required significant capital now needs only initiative, consistency, and willingness to provide value.

## Chapter 4 Quick Win:

List your top five skills, things you're paid for or others compliment. Each could become a side hustle.

5

---

# INVESTMENT MASTERY

Investment transforms money from a depleting resource into a self-multiplying asset. Yet most people never invest beyond employer 401k contributions, if that. They keep savings in accounts paying 0.01% interest while inflation erodes 3% annually, guaranteeing real losses. They fear market volatility while accepting the certainty of inflation's destruction. This hesitation quietly locks people into financial stagnation, even when better options are readily available.

The stock market isn't gambling, despite popular perception. Gambling depends on luck. Investing depends on ownership. While gambling involves negative expected returns where the house always wins, the stock market has positive expected returns because it represents ownership in companies creating real value. When you buy stock, you become a partial owner of businesses that generate profits, develop innovations, and compound value over time. The distinction between investing and gambling is crucial, one builds wealth systematically while the other destroys it.

Understanding investment as business ownership rather than paper trading transforms perspective:

- You're not buying ticker symbols hoping numbers go up,,you're purchasing fractional ownership in real companies
- Apple isn't just AAPL on a screen, it's millions of employees creating products billions of people buy
- Amazon isn't just AMZN, it's warehouses, trucks, cloud servers, and logistics networks serving global commerce
- When you own stock, you own pieces of the economy's productive capacity

The psychological barriers preventing investment are more powerful than financial ones. Fear of losing money paralyzes people into guaranteed losses through inflation. Analysis paralysis keeps them researching forever without acting. Complexity overwhelm makes them believe investing requires expertise it doesn't. These mental barriers must be conquered before wealth building can begin.

## The Janitor Who Out-Invested the Vice President

Ronald Read was a janitor at JCPenney. He pumped gas, swept floors, and lived in a modest Vermont home. His stepchildren had no idea he was rich.

Meanwhile, three floors up from Ronald's mop closet, Vice President Thomas Chen managed his portfolio daily. Harvard MBA. Bloomberg terminal on his desk. He day-traded tech stocks, followed CNBC religiously, and loved telling anyone who'd listen about his "proprietary trading strategy."

When Ronald died in 2014, his will shocked everyone. The janitor left $6 million to his local library and hospital.

The VP? He was still working at 68, his account devastated by trying to time the dot-com bubble, then 2008, then crypto. His "sophisticated" strategy had turned $500,000 into $180,000 over the same period Ronald turned $100,000 into $6 million.

Their secret? Ronald bought index funds every month for 40 years and never sold. That's it.

"But I thought he was just a janitor," his stepson said at the will reading.

The lawyer smiled. "He was. He also understood something most people don't, wealth isn't built by brilliance. It's built by patience."

Ronald started investing in 1970 with $1,000 saved from pumping gas. The market immediately crashed 40%. He kept buying. The 1973 oil crisis hit, down 48%. He kept buying. Black Monday 1987, a 22% single-day apocalypse. Ronald's response? He bought more.

"Weren't you terrified?" his friend once asked during the 2008 crisis as the market fell 57%.

"Of what?" Ronald replied, writing his monthly $300 check to Vanguard. "The market going on sale?"

Thomas, the VP, had a different philosophy. He "bought the dip" in 1999, loading up on tech stocks. Lost 78%. He "called the bottom" in 2007, leveraging into financials. Lost 85%. He "went all in" on crypto in 2021. Lost 90%.

Each time, he'd rebuild with elaborate new strategies, convinced his intelligence would beat the market. Each time, Ronald just kept buying the same boring index fund.

The math was ruthless in its simplicity:

**Ronald's Account:**

- Monthly investment: $300
- Strategy: Buy VTSAX, never sell
- Time: 40 years
- Final value: $6,000,000

**Thomas's Account:**

- Monthly investment: $1,000
- Strategy: Trade, time, pick winners
- Time: 40 years
- Final value: $180,000

At Ronald's funeral, Thomas finally understood. The janitor hadn't won because he was smarter. He won because he wasn't trying to be smart. While Thomas analyzed charts, Ronald cleaned toilets and bought index funds. While Thomas predicted crashes, Ronald lived through them buying steadily. While Thomas sought glory, Ronald sought time.

The inscription on Ronald's library donation reads: "In memory of Ronald Read, who proved wealth is built by those who invest regularly, diversify broadly, and wait patiently."

The janitor who swept floors left millions. The VP who managed portfolios left debt.

## Why the Worst Days Create the Biggest Fortunes

Over any twenty-year period in market history, including the Great Depression, World Wars, stagflation, dot-com bubble, and financial crises, the stock market has never lost money. The worst twenty-year period still produced positive returns. Over thirty-year periods, the worst return was 854%

cumulative, or about 7.8% annually. The average thirty-year period returned 2,109%, or about 10.6% annually.

These aren't projections, hopes, or theories, this is historical fact based on over a century of data:

- **1900-1920:** Including World War I, returned 293% despite global devastation
- **1929-1949:** Including the Great Depression and World War II, returned 244%
- **1962-1982:** The "dead" market with stagflation still returned 373%
- **2000-2020:** Including two major crashes, returned 324%

Yet most people avoid the market because they confuse volatility with risk. Volatility means prices fluctuate. Risk means permanent loss of capital. The market's volatility is the price of admission for superior returns. Those who can tolerate temporary fluctuations get rewarded with long-term wealth multiplication.

Consider the market's resilience through history's worst events:

- **1929 Crash:** Stocks fell 89%, yet patient investors saw new highs within 25 years and 10x returns within 40 years
- **1987 Black Monday:** 22% single-day crash, fully recovered within two years
- **2000 Dot-Com Bubble:** NASDAQ fell 78%, but total market recovered within seven years
- **2008 Financial Crisis:** 57% decline terrified a generation, yet market tripled within a decade

- **2020 COVID Crash:** 34% decline in weeks, new all-time highs within five months

Every crash, crisis, and catastrophe has been followed by recovery and new highs. Betting against this pattern means betting against human innovation and progress.

## Index Fund Revolution

Index fund investing solves the problem of stock selection. Instead of trying to pick winning companies, you buy all of them through a single fund. An S&P 500 index fund owns the five hundred largest American companies. A total market fund owns essentially every public company in America. This diversification eliminates individual company risk while capturing market returns.

The mathematics overwhelmingly favor index funds:

- 95% of professional fund managers fail to beat index funds over fifteen-year periods
- After accounting for fees and taxes, this failure rate approaches 99%
- The average actively managed fund charges 1.0% annually versus 0.03% for index funds
- Over 30 years, that 0.97% fee difference compounds to losing 25% of total returns

These professional managers have Harvard MBAs, Bloomberg terminals, research teams, and full-time dedication to beating the market. If they can't succeed consistently, amateur stock pickers have virtually no chance. Yet millions of investors destroy wealth trying to outsmart the market rather than accepting market returns through index funds.

The beauty of index investing is its simplicity. No research required. No stock picking needed. No market timing necessary. Buy the entire market through one fund, hold forever, and get wealthy slowly but surely. This approach requires no skill, no intelligence, no connections, just patience and discipline. The janitor who invests in index funds builds more wealth than the investment banker who actively trades.

Popular index fund options for building wealth:

- **VTSAX/VTI:** Total U.S. stock market, owning 4,000+ companies
- **VFIAX/VOO:** S&P 500, owning America's 500 largest companies
- **VTIAX/VXUS:** Total international stock market for global diversification
- **VTWAX/VT:** Total world stock market in one fund

## Dollar-Cost Averaging Mastery

Dollar-cost averaging automates investing success. By investing a fixed amount monthly regardless of market conditions, you automatically buy more shares when prices are low and fewer when prices are high. This mathematical averaging reduces your cost basis over time without requiring any market timing skill.

Consider this real example:

- Investing $1,000 monthly when market is at 100: Buy 10 shares
- Market drops to 80: Your $1,000 now buys 12.5 shares

- Market recovers to 100: You own more shares bought at discount
- Market rises to 120: Your discount shares amplify gains

Set up automatic monthly transfers from checking to investment accounts and the system runs itself. This removes emotion from investing, prevents market timing attempts, and ensures consistent wealth building regardless of market conditions. The investor who consistently invests $500 monthly regardless of headlines builds more wealth than one trying to time perfect entry points.

Market timing is a fool's errand that destroys wealth:

- Missing the 10 best days over 20 years cuts returns in half
- Missing the 20 best days eliminates nearly all gains
- Missing the 30 best days produces negative returns
- The best days often immediately follow the worst days
- Those who sell during crashes miss subsequent recoveries

## Tax-Advantaged Account Optimization

Tax-advantaged accounts amplify returns significantly through compound benefits. Traditional 401k contributions reduce current taxable income, providing immediate tax savings that can be invested for additional returns. Roth IRA contributions grow tax-free forever, with no taxes on withdrawals in retirement. HSAs provide triple tax advantages:

deductible contributions, tax-free growth, and tax-free withdrawals for medical expenses.

The optimal investment order maximizes these advantages:

1. **401k to employer match:** 50-100% guaranteed immediate return
2. **HSA maximum ($4,150 individual, $8,300 family):** Triple tax advantage
3. **Roth IRA maximum ($7,000):** Tax-free growth forever
4. **401k maximum ($23,000):** Tax-deferred growth
5. **Taxable accounts:** Only after exhausting tax-advantaged space

Consider the power of these tax advantages. A 25-year-old maximizing tax-advantaged accounts can contribute $34,150 annually (401k: $23,000, IRA: $7,000, HSA: $4,150). Invested at 10% returns, this becomes $23 million by 65. Without tax advantages, the same investments might yield only $15 million after taxes. The $8 million difference represents the value of understanding and utilizing tax-advantaged accounts.

Advanced tax strategies multiply benefits further:

- **Backdoor Roth:** High earners can convert traditional IRA contributions to Roth
- **Mega Backdoor Roth:** Some 401k plans allow after-tax contributions converted to Roth
- **Tax Loss Harvesting:** Sell losers to offset gains, reducing current taxes
- **Asset Location:** Hold tax-inefficient investments in tax-advantaged accounts

## Asset Allocation Mastery

Asset allocation determines returns more than any other factor. The choice between stocks and bonds, domestic and international, large cap and small cap drives ninety percent of portfolio performance. Individual security selection and market timing contribute less than ten percent. Yet most investors focus on picking stocks while ignoring asset allocation.

Age-based allocation frameworks:

- **Age 20-30:** 100% stocks for maximum growth potential
- **Age 30-40:** 90% stocks, 10% bonds for slight stability
- **Age 40-50:** 80% stocks, 20% bonds for balance
- **Age 50-60:** 70% stocks, 30% bonds for protection
- **Age 60+:** 60% stocks, 40% bonds for income

However, with longer lifespans and lower bond yields, many advisors now recommend more aggressive allocations. Some suggest "age minus 20" in bonds, keeping more in stocks longer. The key is choosing an allocation you can maintain through market volatility without panic selling.

Rebalancing maintains target allocation and improves returns:

- Portfolio drift occurs naturally as different assets perform differently
- Annual rebalancing sells what has outperformed to buy what has underperformed
- This systematically sells high and buys low without emotion

- More frequent rebalancing generates unnecessary taxes without meaningful benefit
- Set calendar reminders or use target-date funds for automatic rebalancing

## International Diversification

International diversification reduces risk without sacrificing returns. While American markets have performed well recently, international markets have outperformed in different historical periods. Japan dominated the 1980s. Emerging markets led the 2000s. Europe excelled in various periods. Holding 20-40% international exposure provides diversification benefits and exposure to global growth.

Many excellent companies happen to be headquartered outside America:

- **Technology:** Samsung (Korea), ASML (Netherlands), TSMC (Taiwan)
- **Automotive:** Toyota (Japan), Volkswagen (Germany), BYD (China)
- **Consumer:** Nestle (Switzerland), Unilever (UK), L'Oreal (France)
- **Finance:** HSBC (UK), Allianz (Germany), Ping An (China)

Excluding them creates unnecessary concentration risk. The global economy is interconnected, true diversification requires global exposure.

Emerging markets offer higher growth potential with higher volatility. Countries like China, India, Brazil, and Indonesia have younger populations, growing middle classes, and expanding economies. While riskier than developed markets, a small allocation to emerging markets can enhance returns. A balanced approach might include:

- 60% U.S. stocks for stability and familiarity
- 25% developed international for diversification
- 15% emerging markets for growth potential

The path to investment mastery isn't complex, it's simple but not easy. Buy index funds consistently, hold them forever, maintain appropriate allocation, and ignore market noise. This approach lacks excitement, but it builds extraordinary wealth precisely because it doesn't rely on excitement to work. The difference between financial freedom and perpetual struggle often comes down to starting this simple investment system and maintaining it regardless of market conditions or emotional impulses.

## Chapter 5 Quick Wins:

Read One Investment Book - Start with "A Random Walk Down Wall Street" or "The Bogleheads' Guide to Investing."

**6**

---

# REAL ESTATE WEALTH
# MULTIPLICATION

Real estate has created more millionaires than any other investment vehicle because it generates returns through four distinct mechanisms that compound together:

## The Four Profit Centers:

• **Appreciation**: Properties historically gain 3-5% annually, hot markets see 10-20% yearly

• **Cash Flow**: Monthly profit after expenses, typically $200-500 per property for beginners

• **Mortgage Paydown**: Tenants pay off your loan, adding $200-400 monthly to your net worth

• **Tax Benefits**: Depreciation and deductions save $2,000-10,000 annually per property

**Real Numbers Example**: A $200,000 rental property with 20% down ($40,000 invested) realistically generates:

• Monthly cash flow: $300 ($3,600 annually)

• Annual appreciation at 4%: $8,000 in equity growth

• Principal paydown year one: $3,000

- Tax savings through depreciation: $2,000

Total first-year return: $16,600 on $40,000 invested (41.5% return)

The leverage amplification effect is where things get exciting. Banks won't lend you money to buy stocks, but they'll lend 75-80% for real estate. This means your $40,000 controls a $200,000 asset. When that property appreciates to $250,000, you don't make 25%, you make 125% on your invested capital.

## What Nobody Tells You About Getting Started:

- You don't need perfect credit (620+ for FHA loans, 740+ for best rates)
- You don't need 20% down (3.5% for FHA, 5% for conventional owner-occupied)
- You don't need to be handy (property management costs 8-10% of rent)
- You don't need to quit your job (actually, you need employment for loans)
- You don't need to start big (house hacking your current residence counts)

## THE BUY AND HOLD STRATEGY

Each property typically generates $200-500 monthly profit after all expenses. To replace a $60,000 salary, you need 10-25 properties.

**The 10-year wealth building progression:**

- **Year 1-2:** Buy first property (house hack or small rental), learn the business
- **Year 3-4:** Buy property #2-3 using equity and cash flow from property #1

- **Year 5-6**: Properties #4-6, now generating $1,500-3,000 monthly
- **Year 7-8**: Properties #7-10, crossing $4,000 monthly cash flow
- **Year 9-10**: Optimize portfolio, potentially $5,000+ monthly passive income

**The 70% Rule protects your profits**: Never pay more than 70% of after-repair value minus repair costs.

Example: If a house is worth $200,000 fixed up and needs $30,000 in repairs, pay a maximum of $110,000 (200,000 × 0.70 - 30,000).

**Location Selection Determines Success:**

- **Growth indicators**: Population increasing 1%+ annually, major employers moving in
- **Rent ratios**: Monthly rent should equal 0.7-1.2% of purchase price
- **Neighborhood grades**: B and C neighborhoods balance cash flow and appreciation
- **School ratings**: Properties near 7+ rated schools maintain value and attract quality tenants

## HOUSE HACKING: Live Free While Building Wealth

House hacking can eliminate your largest expense (housing) while building equity and generating income.

**Real House Hacking Income Examples:**

- **Duplex**: Buy for $250,000, live in one side, rent the other for $1,500. Your mortgage is $1,600. Net cost: $100/month versus $1,500 renting
- **Triplex**: Buy for $350,000, rent two units for $1,200 each. Your mortgage is $2,100. You're living free with $300 monthly profit

- **Single Family + Roommates**: Buy 4-bedroom for $300,000, rent 3 rooms at $700 each. Your mortgage is $1,800. Profit: $300 monthly

**Advanced House Hacking Strategies:**

- Furnished room rentals: Charge 30-50% premium for furnished rooms to traveling professionals

- Garage conversion: Convert to studio for $15,000, rent for $800 monthly

- Basement apartment: Finish for $25,000, add $1,200 monthly income

- Airbnb spare rooms: Short-term rentals earn 2x long-term rates

- Live-in flip: Live there 2+ years while renovating, sell tax-free up to $250,000 gain

**The FHA House Hack Blueprint:**

1 Save 3.5% down plus $5,000 for closing costs and reserves

2 Find 2-4 unit property where rents cover 75%+ of mortgage

3 Get FHA loan requiring only 3.5% down

4 Live in worst unit while renting others

5 Fix up your unit using rental cash flow

6 After one year, move out and rent your unit

7 Repeat with new FHA loan

## $200 Rent Increase That Created a Millionaire

Marcus stared at his laptop screen, the email from his landlord still glowing like a taunt. Another rent increase, $200 more per month. At 28, making $52,000 a year, he was exhausted from running on a treadmill that kept getting faster.

"That's it," he muttered, remembering something his

grandfather once said: "Real estate has created more millionaires than anything else. But everyone thinks it's too complicated to start."

With $15,000 saved for a "someday" wedding, Marcus did what his friends called financial suicide. He bought a duplex nobody wanted for $250,000 using an FHA loan, just 3.5% down, roughly $8,750.

The place was hideous. Mustard yellow walls, carpet that might've been white in 1985, and a kitchen that screamed "divorce sale." His friends laughed. His mother cried. But the math was beautiful: live in one side, rent the other for $1,500. His mortgage? $1,600. His new housing cost? Just $100.

Six months of YouTube University, countless Home Depot trips, and more swear words than he'd used in his entire life transformed his side into something respectable. The tenant's rent now covered nearly his entire mortgage. Marcus was essentially living free while building equity.

Year two changed everything. He discovered the BRRRR strategy, Buy, Rehab, Rent, Refinance, Repeat. Using his duplex as collateral, he partnered with a hard money lender to buy a foreclosure for $70,000 cash. The house looked like a crime scene. Six weeks and $25,000 later, it looked like a home.

The appraisal came in at $140,000. He refinanced at 75%, pulled out $105,000, this entire investment plus $10,000 profit, and kept a property that generated $400 monthly in passive income.

His friends stopped laughing. His girlfriend Sarah started asking questions.

By year three, Marcus owned four properties generating $2,200 monthly. Sarah became his business partner, then his wife. That "someday" wedding? Paid for entirely by rental income.

Five years after that crushing rent increase, Marcus stood before a packed classroom at the community college, teaching real estate basics. He clicked to his first slide, that ugly mustard duplex.

"Everyone always asks, 'What's the secret? How much money do you really need?'" He paused, scanning the eager faces. "The secret is starting before you feel ready. I began with $8,750 and a lot of fear. Today, I own 12 properties generating $8,000 monthly. My net worth just crossed $1.2 million."

A hand shot up. "But isn't it risky?"

Marcus smiled, remembering his own trembling finger hovering over the "submit offer" button five years ago.

"You know what's risky? Paying someone else's mortgage forever while they raise your rent every year. Real estate isn't about getting rich quick, it's about getting rich for certain. One property at a time, one rent check at a time."

After class, a young woman approached, determination blazing in her eyes.

"That first duplex, how did you know it was the right one?"

"I didn't," Marcus admitted. "But I knew that doing nothing guaranteed nothing would change. Sometimes the 'perfect' property is just the one you actually buy."

Walking to his car, his phone buzzed. Sarah had sent a photo from their latest renovation, their two-year-old daughter wearing an oversized hard hat, holding a toy hammer.

"Teaching her the family business," the message read.

Marcus smiled. That $200 rent increase had been the push off the cliff he needed. Sometimes the worst moments create the best opportunities, if you're brave enough to jump.

## THE BRRRR STRATEGY

BRRRR (Buy, Rehab, Rent, Refinance, Repeat) enables rapid portfolio growth with limited capital. This is how investors build 10+ property portfolios in 2-3 years starting with just $50,000. The secret? You recycle the same capital repeatedly.

**Real BRRRR Deal with Actual Numbers:**

• **Buy**: Distressed property for $70,000 cash (ARV is $140,000)

• **Rehab**: Invest $25,000 in strategic renovations

• **Rent**: Property now rents for $1,400 monthly

• **Refinance**: Appraises for $140,000, loan at 75% LTV = $105,000

• **Repeat**: You get all $95,000 back plus $10,000 profit to do another deal

**After refinancing, monthly income:**

• Rent collected: $1,400

• Mortgage payment: -$750

• Taxes and insurance: -$250

• Management and maintenance: -$200

• **Monthly cash flow: $200** (infinite return since you have $0 invested)

**Critical BRRRR Success Factors:**

• The 70% Rule is sacred: Never pay more than 70% of ARV minus repairs

• Hard money works: Borrow purchase and rehab costs at 10-12% interest for speed

• Speed matters: Every month of holding costs eats profit, renovate in 4-6 weeks max

- Find reliable contractors before you buy, not after
- Have multiple exit strategies: If refinance fails, can you sell profitably? Rent as-is?

## SHORT-TERM RENTAL OPTIMIZATION

Short-term rentals through Airbnb and VRBO can generate 2-3x traditional rental income. A property renting for $1,500 monthly long-term might generate $4,500 monthly short-term.

**Real Income Breakdown:**

- Traditional rental: $1,500/month, $18,000 annually
- Short-term rental at 65% occupancy: $150/night × 20 nights = $3,000/month
- After expenses (cleaning, supplies, utilities): $2,200 net monthly
- **Annual net income: $26,400 versus $18,000 traditional**
- Additional effort: 5-10 hours monthly with proper systems

**Location Criteria for Profitable STRs:**

- Tourist destinations: Near attractions, beaches, mountains, or entertainment
- Business travel: Close to hospitals, universities, or corporate centers
- Experience proximity: Walking distance to downtown, restaurants, nightlife
- Regulation friendly: Verify local STR laws, many cities ban or restrict them

**The $10,000 Setup for Premium Rates:**

- Professional photography: $500
- Designer furniture and décor: $5,000
- Smart home tech (locks, thermostat): $1,000

- Premium linens and amenities: $1,000
- Unique touches (local art, guides): $500
- Initial supplies and setup: $2,000

**Automation for Passive Income:**
- Smart locks for self check-in (no meeting guests)
- Cleaning service on auto-schedule between guests
- Virtual assistant handles messaging for $200/month
- Dynamic pricing software maximizes revenue

## COMMERCIAL REAL ESTATE: Graduate to Bigger Deals

Commercial real estate offers higher income, longer leases, and less management than residential. Small commercial deals are accessible and often easier than residential.

**Starter Commercial Properties:**

- **Small strip centers**: $300,000-500,000, generating $3,000-5,000 monthly

- **6-10 unit apartments**: Commercial financing, residential simplicity

- **Self-storage facilities**: $500,000 can buy 100 units generating $7,000 monthly

- **Mobile home parks**: $400,000 for 20 pads at $300 each = $6,000 monthly

- **Mixed-use buildings**: Store below, apartments above, multiple income streams

**Why Commercial Beats Residential:**

- **Triple net leases**: Tenants pay taxes, insurance, and maintenance

- **5-10 year leases**: Stable income versus annual residential turnover

- **Annual increases**: Built-in 2-3% annual rent escalations

- **Business tenants:** They maintain property to attract customers
- **Value control:** Increase income by $1,000/month, increase value by $100,000+

## REITs: Real Estate Income Without the Hassles

REITs provide liquid real estate exposure for those not ready for direct ownership. They generate reliable income and appreciation without tenant calls or maintenance issues.

## REIT Income Potential:

- Average REIT dividend yield: 4-6% annually
- High-yield REITs: 7-10% (mortgage REITs, struggling sectors)
- Growth REITs: 2-4% yield but 10-15% annual appreciation

**$100,000 invested: Generates $400-1,000 monthly passive income**

## Strategic REIT Selection:

- **Residential REITs:** Steady 4-5% yields, benefit from housing shortage
- **Industrial/Warehouse REITs:** E-commerce growth driving 15%+ annual returns
- **Healthcare REITs:** Aging population ensures long-term demand
- **Avoid office REITs:** Remote work crushing demand and values

**The Hybrid Strategy:**

1 Start with REITs while learning real estate (generates immediate income)

2 Use REIT dividends to save for first property down payment

3 Transition to direct ownership for better returns

4 Keep some REITs for liquidity and diversification

5 Target combined portfolio generating $10,000+ monthly within 10 years

The path to real estate wealth isn't mysterious, it's mathematical. Whether starting with house hacking, building a rental portfolio, or investing in REITs, real estate provides multiple paths to financial independence. The key is starting with whatever strategy matches your current resources and goals, then systematically expanding as knowledge and capital grow. Every property purchased, every rent check collected, and every mortgage payment made by tenants builds your wealth foundation stone by stone until financial freedom becomes inevitable.

## Chapter 6 Quick Win:

Calculate Your House Hacking Potential - Research duplex prices in your area. Calculate how rental income would offset mortgage costs.

# BUSINESS, ENTREPRENEURSHIP, & STOCK

Building wealth through ownership takes two primary forms: creating your own business or buying shares in existing businesses through the stock market. Both paths lead to wealth, but with dramatically different risk-return profiles, time commitments, and skill requirements. The savvy wealth builder often pursues both simultaneously, using employment or business income to fund stock investments while building entrepreneurial ventures for exponential returns.

Stock market investing provides the simplest path to business ownership. When you buy shares of Apple, Amazon, or Microsoft, you become a partial owner of these businesses without managing operations, hiring employees, or finding customers. The average annual return of the S&P 500 over the past century is approximately 10%, turning $1,000 monthly investments into $2.3 million over 30 years. This passive approach to wealth building requires minimal time and expertise, making it accessible to anyone with investable income.

Building your own business, conversely, provides the highest potential returns of any wealth-building strategy:

- **Stock market returns:** Average 10% annually
- **Successful business returns:** Can generate 100%, 1,000%, or even 10,000% returns
- **Wealth timeline difference:** Financial independence in 30 years (stocks) vs 3 years (business)
- **Value creation example:** Employee saving 20% of $100,000 = $20,000 annually
- **Business owner example:** Building $2 million business in 5 years = $400,000 annual value creation

The optimal strategy combines both approaches:

- Use earned income to invest in diversified stock portfolios for reliable long-term growth
- Simultaneously build businesses for exponential wealth creation
- Reinvest business profits into stocks for diversification and passive income
- Create multiple income streams protecting against single-point failure
- Maximize wealth accumulation through both stability and growth potential

**The Two Mechanics**

Mike and Tony worked at the same auto shop, both earning $60,000 annually. During lunch breaks, they'd dream about owning something instead of just fixing it.

Mike started investing $500 monthly in index funds. "I own a piece of every company in America," he'd say, checking his phone. "Amazon, Google, Tesla, I own them all." His coworkers laughed. "Sure, Mike. All 0.0000001% of them."

Tony had different plans. Evenings and weekends, he fixed cars in his garage, cash only, word-of-mouth marketing. Within a year, he had ten regular customers. Year two: hired his nephew, rented a small shop. Year three: three employees, fifty monthly customers. His side business was netting $8,000 monthly.

Here's where their paths converged brilliantly. Tony took his business profits and dumped them into the same index funds Mike bought. While Mike invested $500 monthly from his salary, Tony invested $5,000 monthly from his business.

Five years later: Mike's portfolio hit $40,000, solid, respectable, on track for retirement at 65. Tony's portfolio reached $400,000, plus he owned a business worth $500,000. Same starting point, same investment strategy, but Tony had discovered the multiplier effect: businesses generate cash that, when invested, creates exponential wealth.

The twist? Mike eventually joined Tony's business as a partner, bringing his investing discipline to the operation. Together, they built a chain of shops while systematically investing every profit dollar. They often joke: "We're not in the car business, we're in the wealth business. Cars just pay for the index funds."

## Understanding Stock Market Fundamentals

Before diving into business creation, it's crucial to understand stock investing as the foundation of passive wealth building. Stocks represent fractional ownership in real companies with real assets, revenues, and profits. When you buy stock, you're not gambling on price movements, you're purchasing a piece of the company's future earnings and growth potential.

The power of index fund investing cannot be overstated:

- **Diversification:** Own hundreds or thousands of companies simultaneously
- **Risk elimination:** No individual company risk while capturing market returns
- **Professional failure rate:** 95% of fund managers fail to beat index funds over 15 years
- **Top index funds:** VTSAX, VOO, VTI provide instant diversification
- **The conclusion:** If Wall Street professionals can't beat the market, individual stock picking becomes gambling

Dollar-cost averaging into index funds provides the most reliable path to stock market wealth:

- Invest a fixed amount monthly regardless of market conditions
- Automatically buy more shares when prices are low, fewer when high
- Remove emotion from investing through mechanical approach
- Set up automatic monthly transfers from checking to investment accounts
- **The math:** $500 monthly invested at 10% returns becomes $1.13 million over 30 years

Individual stock investing guidelines:

- Limit individual stocks to 10-20% of portfolio maximum
- Focus on companies within your "circle of competence"
- Buy businesses whose products you use and understand
- Comprehend the business model and competitive advantages
- Never invest based solely on recommendations or rising prices

## The Entrepreneurial Wealth Equation

Every business fundamentally does one thing: solves problems for profit. The bigger the problem, the more people affected, and the better your solution, the more money you make. This applies whether you're starting your own business or evaluating stocks to purchase. Most aspiring entrepreneurs fail because they focus on their solution rather than the problem. They build products nobody wants, solving problems nobody has, then wonder why nobody buys. Successful entrepreneurs obsess over problems, understanding that solutions without problems are hobbies, not businesses.

The entrepreneurial equation is simple yet powerful: **Value Created × Number of People Served × Price Point = Revenue**

Ways to increase each variable:

- **Value Created:** Solve bigger problems or solve them better than alternatives

- **Number Served:** Superior marketing, distribution, and scalability
- **Price Point:** Target premium markets, add premium features, position uniquely
- **Result:** Master this equation and wealth becomes mathematical rather than mysterious

This same equation applies to evaluating stocks:

- Amazon expanded from books to solving every commerce problem
- Apple moved from computers to smartphones to wearables
- Microsoft evolved from operating systems to cloud services to AI
- Growing revenues indicate solving bigger problems for more people at higher prices

The leverage principle separates true business owners from self-employed individuals:

- **Employees/Freelancers:** Trade time for money linearly (one hour = one hour's pay)
- **Business Owners:** Create systems generating money independent of time
- **Stock Investors:** Leverage other people's time and expertise
- **The Advantage:** Thousands of employees at companies you own work to increase your wealth while you sleep

## Stock Investing While Building Businesses

The journey from employee to entrepreneur doesn't require abandoning stock investing, in fact, stocks provide crucial diversification during the risky business-building phase. Maintain automatic investments in index funds even while pouring energy into business creation. This ensures wealth and asset building continues even if business ventures fail, providing psychological safety that actually increases entrepreneurial risk tolerance.

The barbell strategy for optimal risk-adjusted returns:

- **One end:** Extremely safe investments (index funds) providing steady 10% returns
- **Other end:** Extremely risky but high-reward ventures (your business) with 1,000% potential
- **Avoid:** Middle ground of moderately risky investments with limited upside
- **Result:** Index funds ensure eventual wealth while business enables rapid wealth

Profit reinvestment decision framework:

- **Business returns 50%+:** Reinvest everything back into growth
- **Returns normalize to 20-30%:** Begin diversifying into stocks
- **Mature business:** Transition from concentration to diversification
- **Goal:** Preserve wealth while maintaining growth

Business owners should view public stocks as both competition and opportunity:

- Study public companies in your industry for valuation multiples
- Understand growth strategies and competitive dynamics
- If public companies trade at 5x revenue, that suggests your exit valuation
- Learn from their technology investments and market strategies
- Use public markets as invaluable intelligence for private business

## From Idea to Implementation

Ideas are worthless; execution is everything, this applies equally to starting businesses and investing in stocks. The world is full of brilliant ideas that never generate a dollar because they remain ideas. Meanwhile, mediocre ideas executed brilliantly generate millions.

Examples of execution beating innovation:

- **Facebook:** Wasn't first social network (Friendster, MySpace came first)
- **Google:** Wasn't first search engine (Yahoo, AltaVista preceded it)
- **Amazon:** Wasn't first e-commerce company but executed better
- **Netflix:** Wasn't first streaming service but executed the transition flawlessly

When evaluating stocks, look for execution quality indicators:

- Customer retention rates

- Margin expansion trends
- Market share growth
- Operational efficiency improvements
- Management track record of delivering promises

The minimum viable product (MVP) approach:

- Build the minimum viable product that solves the core problem, launch in weeks, not months
- Test with real customers paying real money
- Use feedback to guide development
- Ensure you build what markets want
- Apply same principle to investing, start with simple index funds before complex strategies

## Service Business Foundations

Service businesses offer the fastest path to cash flow with minimal capital requirements, and profits from service businesses provide excellent funding for stock investments. A consultant generating $10,000 monthly can invest $5,000 in stocks while living on $5,000. Within five years, those stock investments could be worth $400,000, providing passive income that eventually replaces service income.

The power of specialization in services and stocks:

- **Generic service:** "Marketing consultant" charges $50-100/hour
- **Specialized service:** "Facebook ads for cosmetic dentists" charges $200-500/hour
- **Stock parallel:** Sector expertise enables superior stock selection

- **Healthcare knowledge:** Better medical stock picks
- **Technology expertise:** Better software stock evaluation
- **Key insight:** Business expertise becomes investing advantage

## Digital Products and Stock Synergies

Information products scale infinitely with zero marginal cost, similar to software companies that dominate stock market returns. Understanding digital product economics helps identify winning stocks.

Key metrics for digital product companies:

- High gross margins (70%+ ideal)
- Recurring revenue models
- Network effects creating moats
- Low customer acquisition costs
- High customer lifetime values

Examples of digital transformation creating value:

- Adobe's transition from boxed software to cloud subscriptions
- Microsoft's shift to Office 365 and Azure
- Autodesk's move to subscription model
- Each generated spectacular returns for shareholders

Learning from public companies in your space:

- **Course creators:** Study Coursera, Udemy, Chegg

- **Membership sites:** Analyze Netflix, Spotify, Peloton
- **Content creators:** Evaluate Disney, Meta, YouTube
- **Key advantage:** Operational experience provides insights passive investors lack

## SaaS Mastery and Software Stock Selection

SaaS represents the apex of business models, which explains why software stocks have dominated market returns for decades. Understanding SaaS metrics enables better evaluation of software stocks.

Critical SaaS metrics for evaluation:

- **Monthly Recurring Revenue (MRR):** Growth rate and consistency
- **Customer Acquisition Cost (CAC):** Efficiency of growth spending
- **Lifetime Value (LTV):** Revenue per customer over time
- **LTV/CAC Ratio:** Above 3x indicates healthy unit economics
- **Net Revenue Retention:** Above 110% shows expansion within customer base
- **Gross Margins:** Should exceed 70% for true SaaS

Public companies reporting these metrics:

- Salesforce, Shopify, ServiceNow report quarterly
- Understanding operational drivers enables identifying winners

- Low churn and negative churn through upselling predict success
- Efficient customer acquisition indicates scalability
- Your SaaS experience provides evaluation advantage

## E-commerce Empires and Retail Stock Investing

E-commerce enables selling physical products globally with minimal infrastructure, and understanding e-commerce operations provides advantages in retail stock investing.

E-commerce metrics that matter:

- **Conversion rates:** Industry standard 2-3%, leaders achieve 5%+
- **Customer acquisition cost:** Must be profitable on first purchase or within 90 days
- **Average order value:** Higher AOV improves unit economics
- **Repeat purchase rate:** 20%+ indicates product-market fit
- **Fulfillment efficiency:** Same-day/next-day becoming table stakes

Direct-to-consumer (DTC) investment opportunities:

- Warby Parker, Allbirds, and other DTC brands going public
- Your operational experience enables better evaluation

- Understanding unit economics provides investment edge
- Knowing scalability challenges helps identify winners
- Experience with platform dependencies reveals risks

## Content Creation and Media Stock Opportunities

Content creators understand attention economics, making them better media stock investors. Your experience building audiences, monetizing content, and understanding platform dynamics provides insights into companies like Disney, Netflix, and Meta.

Creator economy insights for investing:

- Which platforms are gaining or losing creator attention
- Which monetization models actually work
- Understanding algorithm changes and their impacts
- Recognizing platform risk and diversification needs
- Knowing true engagement versus vanity metrics

The consistency principle:

- **Content creation:** Regular posting beats sporadic perfection
- **Stock investing:** Consistent monthly investing beats market timing

- **Audience building:** Small daily gains compound exponentially
- **Portfolio growth:** Regular contributions create extraordinary results
- **Key lesson:** Consistency over perfection in both domains

## Scaling Through Systems and Portfolio Management

Systems and automation enable scaling both businesses and investment portfolios. Just as you document business processes for delegation, create investment policy statements defining asset allocation, rebalancing triggers, and selection criteria.

Automation priorities for investors:

- Automatic monthly contributions to investment accounts
- Rebalancing triggers when allocation drifts 5%+ from targets
- Tax loss harvesting in taxable accounts
- Dividend reinvestment for compounding
- Bill pay ensuring investment happens first

The progression from operator to owner:

- **Beginner stage:** Manage everything personally
- **Intermediate stage:** Automate routine tasks
- **Advanced stage:** Delegate to advisors while maintaining strategic control
- **Master stage:** Systems run without you

- **Application:** Works for both businesses and portfolios

## The Synergy of Business and Stock Building

The ultimate wealth strategy combines business building with stock investing in a synergistic cycle. Build businesses for explosive growth. Invest profits in stocks for diversification and passive income. Use stock returns to fund new business ventures. Let each success compound into the next opportunity.

Why entrepreneurs become successful investors:

- Charlie Munger built law practice before partnering with Buffett
- Peter Lynch managed Magellan after working in textiles and metals
- Business experience provides pattern recognition
- Operational knowledge creates analytical frameworks
- Understanding of value creation transfers to investing

Tax optimization through combination:

- **Business advantages:** Deduct expenses, equipment, home office
- **Stock advantages:** Long-term capital gains at preferential rates
- **Retirement accounts:** Tax-deferred or tax-free growth
- **Strategic combination:** Can reduce lifetime taxes by millions

- **Key strategy:** Flow business income through tax-advantaged investment accounts

The wealth multiplication formula:

- Business income funds living expenses and investments
- Stock investments provide passive income and diversification
- Passive income eventually replaces business income need
- Freedom to pursue only interesting business ventures
- Wealth compounds from multiple sources simultaneously

The path forward is clear: combine the explosive potential of business ownership with the reliable growth of stock investing. This dual approach provides both the excitement of entrepreneurship and the security of diversified investments, creating multiple paths to financial independence while protecting against any single failure.

## Chapter 7 Quick Wins:

Calculate Your Ownership Goals - Write: "I will own $____ in stocks and a business worth $____ by [date]." Work backward to determine monthly investment needed and business milestones required.

# 8

## THE BITCOIN REVOLUTION

Bitcoin isn't just another investment, it's a complete reimagining of money itself. Launched in 2009 by the pseudonymous Satoshi Nakamoto, Bitcoin solved a problem that computer scientists had wrestled with for decades: creating digital scarcity without requiring trust in any central authority. This breakthrough represents the most significant advance in monetary technology since the invention of paper currency, fundamentally altering how humanity can store, transfer, and conceptualize value in the digital age.

The Byzantine Generals' Problem, which Bitcoin elegantly solved, had stumped computer scientists since the 1980s. The challenge was creating consensus in a distributed system where participants couldn't trust each other and where some might be malicious. Bitcoin's proof-of-work consensus mechanism provided the solution, enabling thousands of independent nodes to agree on a single version of truth without any central coordinator. This innovation transcends currency, it's a breakthrough in distributed systems that will enable countless future applications.

For the first time in human history, we have money that:

- Cannot be printed by any government or central bank
- Cannot be censored or blocked by any authority
- Cannot be confiscated if properly secured
- Cannot be stopped by any government or corporation
- Operates on mathematical rules rather than political whims

While politicians can print trillions of dollars, euros, or yen at will, nobody can create even one additional Bitcoin beyond the predetermined supply schedule coded into its DNA. This makes Bitcoin the hardest money ever invented, harder than gold, harder than real estate, exponentially harder than fiat currency.

The implications cascade across every aspect of economics and society:

- Every fiat currency in history has eventually failed, with an average lifespan of just 27 years
- The dollar has lost 96% of its purchasing power since the Federal Reserve's creation in 1913
- The British pound, once the world's reserve currency, has lost 99.5% of its value since 1900
- Meanwhile, Bitcoin has appreciated from essentially zero to over $60,000 per coin
- Early adopters who bought Bitcoin for pennies have seen returns of 10,000,000% or more, gains

that dwarf every other investment in recorded history

## The Pizza That Cost $800 Million

On May 22, 2010, Laszlo Hanyecz made history. He bought two Papa John's pizzas for 10,000 Bitcoin, the first real-world Bitcoin transaction. Those pizzas cost him about $41.

Everyone laughed. "Imagine paying with fake internet money!"

The pizza shop owner immediately sold the Bitcoin for dollars. "Interesting experiment, but I need real money."

Laszlo's programmer friends debated endlessly. Half thought he was genius for proving Bitcoin worked. Half thought he was foolish for "wasting" Bitcoin on pizza.

By 2013, those 10,000 Bitcoin were worth $1 million. The forums exploded: "The million-dollar pizza!" Laszlo shrugged. "Without that pizza, Bitcoin might never have become real."

By 2017: $200 million worth of pizza. By 2021: $690 million. Today: Over $600 million.

But here's what everyone misses: Laszlo kept mining and buying Bitcoin. He understood something others didn't, you don't need to catch the absolute bottom. You just need to participate.

The pizza shop owner? Still running his shop, still taking only dollars. The friend who called it "fake money"? Still waiting for Bitcoin to "crash to zero." The programmer who bought 100 Bitcoin after seeing the pizza purchase? Retired at 35.

Every technology has its "pizza moment" when visionaries use it while skeptics mock. The internet had people sending emails while others insisted fax machines were sufficient. Bitcoin's pizza moment has passed. The only question now is whether you'll be telling stories about buying at $60,000 or explaining why you waited for "a better entry point" that never came.

## Understanding Bitcoin's Revolutionary Properties

Bitcoin's genius lies in its unique combination of properties that no previous form of money achieved simultaneously. It's scarce like gold but divisible down to one hundred millionth of a Bitcoin, called a satoshi. This extreme divisibility means Bitcoin can function equally well if worth $1 or $1 million per coin, you simply transact in smaller units. It's portable like digital dollars but requires no bank or payment processor to validate transactions. You can carry a fortune across borders in your mind by memorizing a seed phrase, something impossible with gold, cash, or traditional assets.

The verification process showcases Bitcoin's elegance:

- Any participant can validate the entire monetary supply and transaction history using basic computer hardware
- Try auditing the Federal Reserve or Fort Knox's gold reserves, it's impossible for ordinary citizens
- With Bitcoin, every transaction ever made is visible on the public blockchain
- This verifiability eliminates the need for trust in institutions that have repeatedly proven untrustworthy

Bitcoin's anti-fragility grows stronger through adversity.

Every attack, whether from hackers, governments, or critics, has ultimately strengthened the network. The 2017 scaling debate led to improved second-layer solutions like Lightning Network. China's mining ban in 2021 improved geographic distribution of hash power. Each challenge overcome adds to Bitcoin's Lindy effect, the longer it survives, the longer it's likely to continue surviving.

The 21 million Bitcoin supply cap stands as absolutely immutable, written into code that tens of thousands of nodes worldwide enforce. This predictable monetary policy contrasts sharply with fiat currencies, where central banks change policies based on political pressure, economic conditions, or mere whims. When you hold Bitcoin, you know exactly what percentage of total supply you own, and that percentage can never be diluted through monetary expansion. If you own 1 Bitcoin today, you own 1/21,000,000th of all Bitcoin that will ever exist. In fifty years, you'll still own exactly 1/21,000,000th. No government can print more to bail out banks, fund wars, or buy votes.

Bitcoin's decentralization means it has no single point of failure:

- The network consists of hundreds of thousands of nodes spread across every continent
- Nodes run in data centers, homes, even satellites orbiting Earth
- This distribution makes Bitcoin essentially indestructible
- Nuclear war, solar flares, or natural disasters might damage the network temporarily
- As long as even a few nodes survive, Bitcoin continues

Governments have tried banning Bitcoin numerous times, China has "banned" it at least eight times, yet the network continues growing stronger. You can't ban mathematics, you can't prohibit cryptography, and you can't stop people from transmitting information.

## The Network Effect Phenomenon

Metcalfe's Law states that a network's value grows proportionally to the square of its users. Bitcoin exemplifies this principle perfectly. Each new user adds value not just through their own participation but by increasing the network's utility for every existing user. With hundreds of millions of users worldwide and growing, Bitcoin's network effect has reached escape velocity, the point where its dominance becomes self-reinforcing and virtually insurmountable.

The developer ecosystem surrounding Bitcoin continues expanding exponentially:

- Thousands of the world's brightest programmers contribute to Bitcoin's core protocol
- Hundreds of developers build applications on the Lightning Network alone
- Payment channels enable instant, nearly free Bitcoin transactions
- Innovations like Taproot and Schnorr signatures improve privacy and efficiency
- Each improvement makes Bitcoin more useful, attracting more users and developers in a virtuous cycle

Liquidity breeds liquidity in financial markets. Bitcoin's

superior liquidity compared to other cryptocurrencies creates a self-reinforcing advantage. Large investors need deep, liquid markets to enter and exit positions without massive price impact. Bitcoin's $1+ trillion market capitalization and billions in daily volume provide this liquidity. As institutional money flows increase, they naturally gravitate toward Bitcoin's deeper markets, further enhancing its liquidity advantage over competitors.

The Lindy effect suggests that technologies and ideas that have survived longer are likely to continue surviving. Bitcoin, as the first and longest-running cryptocurrency, benefits enormously from this principle. Every day Bitcoin continues operating strengthens confidence in its continued operation. Newer cryptocurrencies claiming superiority must overcome not just Bitcoin's technical features but its proven track record of survival through bear markets, regulatory attacks, technical challenges, and competitive threats.

## The Four-Year Halving Cycle: Your Wealth-Building Timeline

Bitcoin's supply schedule follows a predictable four-year cycle that has historically driven massive price appreciation. Every 210,000 blocks, approximately four years, the reward for mining new blocks cuts in half. This "halving" reduces the rate of new Bitcoin creation, making existing Bitcoin progressively scarcer. The pattern has been remarkably consistent: accumulation phase, halving event, supply shock, price explosion, correction, then repeat at higher levels.

The mathematics behind halving create inevitable supply shocks:

- Currently, miners produce approximately 900 Bitcoin daily
- After the next halving, this drops to 450 Bitcoin daily
- Meanwhile, institutional buyers like MicroStrategy often purchase 1,000+ Bitcoin in single transactions
- The supply-demand imbalance becomes extreme
- When new supply can't meet demand, price must rise to incentivize existing holders to sell

Historical patterns reveal stunning consistency:

- **First halving (2012):** Bitcoin rose from $12 to $1,000, an 83x increase
- **Second halving (2016):** Price surged from $650 to $20,000, a 30x increase
- **Third halving (2020):** Catalyzed rise from $8,000 to $69,000, an 8.6x increase
- **Future projection:** Conservative estimates suggest next cycle could reach $150,000 to $500,000

The psychological impact of halvings extends beyond pure mathematics. They serve as Schelling points, focal points for coordination without communication. Investors worldwide anticipate halvings, creating self-fulfilling prophecies as accumulation increases in anticipation. Media coverage of halvings introduces new participants to Bitcoin's fixed supply narrative. Each halving becomes a global advertisement for Bitcoin's superior monetary policy compared to infinitely printable fiat currencies.

Understanding this cycle transforms Bitcoin from

volatile speculation into strategic accumulation opportunity. The key is to accumulate during the bear markets when pessimism peaks and hold through bull markets when euphoria reigns. Those who bought Bitcoin at the 2017 peak of $20,000 and held are now up over 300%. Those who bought at the 2013 peak of $1,000 are up 6,000%. Every previous all-time high has eventually become a floor that Bitcoin never revisits. This pattern suggests today's prices, which might seem high, will appear laughably cheap in retrospect.

## Institutional Adoption: The Stampede Has Begun

The transition from retail speculation to institutional adoption marks Bitcoin's evolution from experimental technology to established asset class. This shift fundamentally changes Bitcoin's trajectory, bringing trillions in capital, professional custody solutions, regulatory clarity, and mainstream legitimacy. The infrastructure being built today will support Bitcoin's growth for decades.

Corporate adoption is accelerating exponentially:

- **MicroStrategy:** Holds over 190,000 Bitcoin worth billions, using convertible bonds to acquire more
- **Tesla:** Maintains Bitcoin on its balance sheet as treasury asset
- **Block (Square):** Holds thousands of Bitcoin and continues accumulating
- **Strategy shift:** Companies recognize Bitcoin as superior to cash being debased at unprecedented rates

- **Inspiration effect:** Hundreds of companies following early adopters' lead

Nation-state adoption has begun with El Salvador making Bitcoin legal tender and accumulating national Bitcoin reserves. Panama, Ukraine, and Paraguay are exploring similar initiatives. When nations compete for Bitcoin reserves as they once competed for gold reserves, the geopolitical implications will be profound. Countries with Bitcoin reserves will have harder money than those without, creating pressure for universal adoption. The game theory dynamics make widespread sovereign adoption virtually inevitable.

Traditional financial infrastructure now encompasses Bitcoin throughout:

- **Major banks:** JPMorgan, Goldman Sachs, and Morgan Stanley offer Bitcoin services
- **Asset managers:** Fidelity ($11 trillion AUM) provides Bitcoin custody and trading
- **BlackRock:** World's largest asset manager ($10 trillion AUM) launched Bitcoin products
- **Impact:** When firms managing tens of trillions embrace Bitcoin, capital flow becomes torrential

Bitcoin ETFs have transformed accessibility for traditional investors. These products enable Bitcoin exposure through standard brokerage accounts, IRAs, and 401(k)s. The infrastructure removes technical barriers that previously prevented institutional allocation. Pension funds, endowments, and insurance companies can now add Bitcoin exposure while maintaining their existing operational frameworks. Each new access point multiplies potential demand.

## The Mathematical Case for $1 Million Bitcoin

The case for $1 million Bitcoin isn't hopium, it's mathematical inevitability based on monetary dynamics and adoption curves. Let's examine the numbers:

Global wealth distribution and Bitcoin's potential market share:

- **Global wealth total:** Approximately $900 trillion
- **Gold market cap:** $15 trillion
- **Global real estate:** Worth $380 trillion
- **Offshore banking:** Holds $35 trillion
- **Bond markets:** Exceed $130 trillion
- **Bitcoin's opportunity:** Capturing even small percentages drives massive price appreciation

If Bitcoin captures just gold's current market cap, each Bitcoin will be worth $750,000. This seems conservative given Bitcoin's superiority to gold in every monetary dimension except history. Bitcoin is more portable, divisible, verifiable, and scarce than gold. Digital natives who've grown up with smartphones have no emotional attachment to shiny rocks. They'll choose programmable, transportable, divisible Bitcoin over heavy, cumbersome metal that requires expensive storage and verification.

The denominator effect accelerates Bitcoin's fiat price appreciation:

- Central banks print currency to fund deficits, bail out banks, and stimulate economies

- Fiat currency supply expands exponentially
- Bitcoin's fixed supply means its price in debasing currencies must rise proportionally
- If dollars in circulation double, Bitcoin's dollar price doubles even without increased adoption
- The Federal Reserve's balance sheet expanded from $4 trillion to $9 trillion in just two years

Corporate treasury adoption could drive Bitcoin well beyond $1 million:

- **Apple:** Holds $200 billion in depreciating cash
- **Microsoft:** Holds $150 billion losing value to inflation
- **Google:** Holds $140 billion in melting fiat
- **Impact:** If top 100 corporations converted 10% of cash to Bitcoin, they'd need 2 million Bitcoin— 10% of total supply

The insurance and pension fund allocation represents another massive demand driver. These institutions manage approximately $50 trillion globally. A conservative 1% allocation would require $500 billion in Bitcoin purchases, nearly half the current market cap. A 5% allocation would overwhelm available supply. These institutions move slowly but inevitably toward assets that preserve purchasing power. Bitcoin's track record of outperforming every traditional asset class makes allocation decisions increasingly obvious.

## The Technology Stack Revolution

Lightning Network represents Bitcoin's scaling solution that enables instant, nearly free transactions while maintaining the security of the base layer. This second-layer protocol allows millions of transactions per second, rivaling Visa's capacity while maintaining Bitcoin's decentralization. Coffee purchases, streaming payments, and micropayments become practical, expanding Bitcoin's utility from store of value to medium of exchange.

Technical improvements continuously enhance Bitcoin's capabilities:

- **Taproot and Schnorr signatures:** Enhanced privacy and efficiency
- **Complex smart contracts:** Enabled while appearing as regular transactions
- **Privacy improvements:** Protect users from surveillance while maintaining transparency
- **Development pipeline:** Covenants, vaults, and enhanced scripting expand programmability
- **Sidechains:** Liquid and RSK enable experimentation without risking main chain

The conservative, methodical approach to Bitcoin development prioritizes security and decentralization over rapid feature addition, a strategy that has proven wise as competing cryptocurrencies suffer hacks, outages, and centralization.

Integration with existing financial systems accelerates through:

- APIs and payment processors enabling seamless Bitcoin transactions
- Banking partnerships bridging traditional and cryptocurrency worlds

- Companies like Strike enabling instant global payments using Bitcoin rails
- Users interact with familiar currency interfaces while Bitcoin operates underneath
- This abstraction layer provides Bitcoin's benefits without requiring technical understanding

## Global Macro Trends Supporting Bitcoin

The global monetary system faces unprecedented challenges that make Bitcoin's adoption not just likely but necessary:

Debt crisis driving Bitcoin adoption:

- **Global debt:** Exceeds $300 trillion, nearly 400% of global GDP
- **Sustainability:** Governments cannot repay these debts honestly
- **Solution:** They must inflate debts away through currency debasement
- **Bitcoin's role:** Provides the exit door from this doomed system

Negative real interest rates punish savers and reward debtors, inverting traditional economic incentives. When bank deposits lose purchasing power after accounting for inflation, capital seeks alternatives. Bitcoin, with its fixed supply and growing adoption, provides the obvious solution. The longer negative real rates persist, the more capital flows from melting fiat currencies into appreciating Bitcoin.

Geopolitical factors accelerating adoption:

- **Instability:** Regional conflicts and great power competition increase
- **Neutrality:** Bitcoin isn't controlled by America, China, or any nation
- **Reserve asset:** Ideal for countries seeking independence from dollar hegemony
- **Multipolar world:** Requires multipolar money, Bitcoin fits perfectly

Demographic transitions favor Bitcoin adoption:

- Millennials and Gen Z will inherit $68 trillion from Baby Boomers
- Younger generations show strong preference for digital assets
- Surveys consistently show favorable views of Bitcoin over gold or stocks
- As wealth transfers between generations, allocation preferences shift dramatically

Central bank digital currencies (CBDCs) paradoxically accelerate Bitcoin adoption. As governments implement CBDCs enabling total surveillance and control, freezing accounts, implementing negative rates, restricting purchases —demand for financial privacy and sovereignty increases. Bitcoin provides the antidote to CBDC tyranny, offering permissionless, private, sovereign money that governments cannot control.

## Your Strategic Bitcoin Accumulation Plan

The optimal Bitcoin strategy prioritizes consistent accumulation over market timing. Here's your actionable framework:

Dollar-cost averaging implementation:

- **Remove emotion:** Automatic purchases ensure discipline regardless of sentiment
- **Consistency matters:** Whether $50 weekly or $5,000 monthly
- **Platform selection:** Coinbase, Kraken, or Swan Bitcoin for automated purchases
- **Fear advantage:** Accumulate most during crashes when Bitcoin is cheapest

Position sizing guidelines based on personal situation:

- **Young investors (20-35):** Consider 25-50% allocation with long time horizons
- **Middle-aged (35-50):** Balance with 10-20% allocation for growth and stability
- **Near-retirement (50+):** Limit to 5-10% focusing on capital preservation
- **Starting point:** Begin with psychologically comfortable amount, increase with understanding

Storage security best practices:

- **Under $1,000:** Reputable exchanges provide adequate security
- **$1,000-$10,000:** Hardware wallets (Ledger, Trezor, Coldcard) essential
- **$10,000+:** Never store on exchanges long-term "not your keys, not your coins"

- **Life-changing amounts:** Multi-signature setups requiring multiple keys for access
- **Redundancy:** Multiple secure backups of seed phrases in different locations

Tax optimization strategies:

- Hold over one year for long-term capital gains treatment
- Consider Bitcoin IRAs for tax-deferred or tax-free growth
- Understand local tax laws and structure holdings appropriately
- Proper planning means keeping 50-80% of gains versus losing half to taxes

Risk management principles:

- Never invest money needed within five years
- Avoid leverage, volatility can trigger liquidations
- Don't try trading, 95% of traders underperform holders
- Focus on accumulation and long-term holding
- Ignore short-term price movements and media hysteria

## The Lightning Network Revolution

Lightning Network solves Bitcoin's scalability limitations while maintaining decentralization and security. This second-layer solution enables millions of transactions per second at negligible cost, making Bitcoin practical for everyday payments. Coffee purchases, online subscriptions, and even streaming money become possible, expanding Bitcoin's utility beyond store of value to genuine medium of exchange.

Technical architecture enabling scale:

- Payment channels settle on Bitcoin's base layer only when opened or closed
- Between opening and closing, unlimited transactions occur instantly off-chain
- Maintains Bitcoin's security for final settlement
- Enables speed and low cost necessary for commerce
- Major companies like Twitter and Substack have integrated Lightning payments

Network growth metrics showing adoption:

- **Capacity:** Exceeds 3,000 Bitcoin locked in channels
- **Nodes:** Thousands globally strengthening the network
- **Success rate:** Payment reliability exceeding 99% for well-connected nodes
- **Commercial viability:** Infrastructure maturity enabling business applications
- **Future potential:** Replacing traditional payment rails globally

## The Future of Finance

Bitcoin represents more than just a new asset class, it's the foundation for an entirely new financial system:

Programmable money applications:

- Smart contracts automating complex financial arrangements
- Decentralized identity systems providing financial access to billions
- Micropayments enabling new business models
- Machine-to-machine transactions in IoT economy
- Innovations that will transform finance as the internet transformed communication

Convergence with exponential technologies:

- **Artificial Intelligence:** Optimizing trading strategies and wallet security
- **Internet of Things:** Devices transacting autonomously using Bitcoin
- **Virtual Reality:** Metaverses using Bitcoin as native currency
- **Renewable Energy:** Projects monetizing excess capacity through mining
- **Synergy effect:** Each intersection creates new use cases and demand

Bitcoin's societal impact extends beyond finance:

- Separation of money and state matching church-state separation importance
- Governments must fund through transparent taxation, not money printing
- Wars become harder to finance without monetary expansion
- Corruption reduced through publicly auditable transactions

- Power structures existing for centuries
  fundamentally altered

## Seizing the Opportunity of a Lifetime

Bitcoin represents the asymmetric opportunity of our generation:

- **Downside:** Limited to 100% loss if Bitcoin
  completely fails
- **Upside:** 100x or 1,000x returns as global reserve
  currency
- **Historical parallel:** Railroads (1860s),
  automobiles (1900s), internet (1990s)
- **Current opportunity:** Bitcoin today represents
  similar generational wealth potential

We remain remarkably early in Bitcoin's adoption curve:

- Less than 5% of global population owns any
  Bitcoin
- Most institutions haven't allocated yet
- Most corporations haven't added Bitcoin to
  treasuries
- Most governments haven't accumulated reserves
- When these dominoes fall, demand overwhelms
  strictly limited supply

The window for accumulating Bitcoin at these prices won't remain open indefinitely:

- Every day delayed is compound appreciation
  foregone

- Every cycle missed is a 10x multiple lost
- The cost of waiting isn't linear but exponential
- Those who act while others debate build generational wealth

Your financial future depends on decisions made today. Bitcoin provides the vehicle, the mathematics are irrefutable, the trend is unmistakable. The only variable is your participation. Will you seize this opportunity to front-run the greatest monetary transition in human history? Or will you watch from the sidelines as others build generational wealth through Bitcoin? The choice, and the opportunity, is yours to make.

## Chapter 8 Quick Wins:

Learn One Bitcoin Concept Daily - Spend 10 minutes daily learning about blockchain, mining, wallets, or Bitcoin economics. Knowledge builds conviction.

# LIFE INSURANCE AS WEALTH TOOL

Life insurance is the most misunderstood and underutilized wealth building tool available to average investors. While most people see life insurance as a death benefit, a necessary evil to protect dependents, sophisticated investors use certain types of life insurance as tax-free wealth accumulation vehicles, providing benefits far beyond simple death protection. The wealthy have used these strategies for generations while the middle class remains unaware, missing opportunities for tax-free growth, creditor protection, and generational wealth transfer.

The fundamental misconception about life insurance stems from conflating all types into a single category. Term life insurance is indeed pure death protection, but permanent life insurance products function as hybrid investment-protection vehicles. Whole life insurance and indexed universal life insurance (IUL) can function as tax-advantaged investment accounts when structured properly. These policies build cash value that grows tax-deferred, can be accessed tax-free through loans, and passes to heirs income tax-free. Unlike qualified retirement accounts with contribution limits and restrictions, properly structured life insurance has no contribution limits and provides complete flexibility.

Consider the tax advantages that make life insurance unique among investment vehicles:

- Contributions grow tax-deferred like traditional retirement accounts
- Withdrawals up to basis (premiums paid) come out tax-free
- Loans against cash value are tax-free and never require repayment during life
- Death benefits pass to heirs completely income tax-free
- No other investment vehicle combines all these tax advantages

A properly structured policy can provide tax-free income in retirement, emergency access during life, and tax-free legacy at death, a triple tax advantage unavailable elsewhere.

The creditor protection aspects of life insurance add another layer of value rarely discussed:

- In many states, life insurance cash values are completely protected from creditors, lawsuits, and bankruptcy
- This protection makes life insurance valuable for professionals vulnerable to litigation, doctors, lawyers, business owners
- While IRAs and 401(k)s offer some creditor

protection, life insurance often provides superior asset protection depending on state law
- This protection extends to beneficiaries, who receive death benefits shielded from their creditors in most cases

## The Infinite Banking Concept

The infinite banking concept uses whole life insurance to "become your own banker," transforming insurance from expense to financial control system. Instead of paying interest to banks for mortgages, car loans, or credit cards, you borrow from your policy's cash value for major purchases, investments, or opportunities. The policy continues earning dividends even on loaned amounts, you don't interrupt compound growth. You pay yourself back with interest, recapturing what would have been bank profits. This strategy requires significant cash flow but provides unmatched financial flexibility for those who can afford it.

Understanding the mechanics reveals the power of infinite banking:

- When you borrow from your policy, you're actually borrowing from the insurance company using your cash value as collateral
- Your cash value continues earning guaranteed interest plus dividends
- If the policy earns 5% and you pay 6% loan interest, the insurance company makes 1%
- You're paying that interest to yourself, recapturing the full 6%
- Over time, you recapture all the interest you

would have paid to banks while your policy continues compounding

The velocity of money principle amplifies infinite banking benefits. Traditional savings sit idle until spent, generating single use. Money in whole life policies can be used repeatedly through loans while the collateral continues growing. You might borrow for a car, pay yourself back over three years, then borrow again for home improvements. The same dollars provide multiple uses while growing continuously. This velocity multiplication can double or triple the effective return on premium dollars over decades.

Real-world applications demonstrate infinite banking's versatility:

- **Business owners:** Use policy loans for equipment purchases, avoiding bank qualification requirements and maintaining privacy
- **Real estate investors:** Access policy funds for down payments, moving faster than competitors waiting for bank approval
- **Parents:** Fund college education through policy loans, avoiding student loan interest and qualification requirements
- **Retirees:** Create tax-free income through policy loans that never require repayment, optimizing Social Security taxation and Medicare premiums

The psychological benefits of infinite banking extend beyond mathematics:

- Knowing you have immediate access to capital without bank approval provides confidence to seize opportunities
- The discipline of paying yourself back builds wealth systematically
- The privacy of borrowing from yourself rather than banks protects business strategies
- The control over your financial system reduces stress and increases options
- These intangible benefits often exceed the mathematical advantages

## The Two Partners' Different Paths

In 1995, business partners Jack and Robert each bought life insurance when their consulting firm landed its first major contract.

Jack bought a $1 million term policy for $50 monthly. "Insurance is insurance," he said. "Buy the cheapest and invest the difference." He invested his savings in the stock market, riding the dot-com boom, then the crash, then the housing boom, then that crash. His portfolio swung wildly, up 40%, down 50%, up again, down again.

Robert bought a whole life policy, paying $500 monthly. His colleagues mocked him. "You're getting a 4% return when the market's doing 20%!" During the dot-com boom, they showed him their Nasdaq gains. He kept paying premiums.

Fast forward twenty-five years:

Jack's term insurance expired. At 55, new coverage costs $800 monthly for far less death benefit. His investment account, after two major crashes and emotional selling at the worst times, sits at $400,000. His tax bill on withdrawals will be substantial.

Robert has $500,000 in cash value, accessible tax-free through loans. His death benefit has grown to $1.5 million. During the 2008 crisis, while Jack was selling stocks at losses, Robert borrowed $100,000 from his policy to buy rental properties at foreclosure prices. Those properties now generate $3,000 monthly in passive income.

The revelation came at their firm's anniversary dinner. Jack said, "I followed all the conventional advice, buy term and invest the difference."

Robert replied, "So did I. I just defined 'invest' differently."

## Whole Life Insurance Architecture

Whole life insurance provides guaranteed growth, guaranteed death benefit, and potential dividends from mutual insurance companies. The guarantees make whole life the most conservative permanent insurance, appealing to risk-averse investors seeking predictable accumulation. Mutual companies are owned by policyholders, not shareholders, aligning interests toward maximizing policyholder benefits rather than corporate profits.

Properly structuring whole life for cash value accumulation requires specific design elements often opposite to what insurance agents typically recommend:

- Minimize the base death benefit to the lowest amount allowed by the IRS while maintaining life insurance status
- Maximize paid-up additions (PUA) riders that

buy additional paid-up insurance, accelerating cash value growth
- Include riders allowing flexible premium payments
- This structure front-loads cash value accumulation, providing liquidity and growth rather than maximum death benefit

The dividend component of participating whole life provides non-guaranteed but historically consistent returns:

- Major mutual insurers have paid dividends for over 100 consecutive years
- Dividends paid through the Great Depression, World Wars, and financial crises
- Current dividend rates range from 5-6% tax-free, competitive with bonds but without interest rate risk
- Dividends can purchase additional insurance to accelerate compound growth, or they can be taken as cash for income

Guaranteed cash value growth provides the foundation that dividends enhance. Even without dividends, whole life policies guarantee specific cash values at future dates. This guarantee enables precise financial planning impossible with market-based investments. You know exactly how much cash value you'll have in 10, 20, or 30 years minimum, with dividends providing upside. This certainty makes whole life valuable for specific future obligations like college funding or retirement income.

## Indexed Universal Life Innovation

Indexed Universal Life (IUL) insurance links cash value growth to stock market indexes while providing downside protection through floors. When the index rises, your cash value captures gains up to a cap (typically 10-13%). When the index falls, your floor (usually 0%) prevents losses. This asymmetric return profile, participating in gains while avoiding losses, creates compelling long-term growth potential superior to traditional whole life but with more variability.

The mathematics of avoiding losses prove more powerful than most investors realize:

- A portfolio losing 50% requires 100% gain to break even
- IUL policies with 0% floors never face this mathematical disadvantage
- Over time, avoiding losses matters more than capturing maximum gains
- Historical backtesting shows IUL strategies often outperform direct market investment after accounting for taxes and downside protection

IUL flexibility exceeds whole life in premium payments and death benefits:

- Vary premiums based on cash flow
- Skip payments using accumulated values to cover costs
- Accelerate funding when advantageous
- Increase death benefits when needs grow

- Decrease benefits to minimize costs and maximize accumulation
- This flexibility makes IUL attractive for business owners and those with variable income

The living benefit riders available with IUL provide additional value beyond accumulation and death benefits:

- **Chronic illness riders:** Allow accessing death benefits if unable to perform activities of daily living
- **Critical illness riders:** Provide lump sums upon diagnosis of covered conditions
- **Long-term care riders:** Convert death benefits to monthly care payments
- **Terminal illness riders:** Access death benefits early if diagnosed with terminal condition
- These riders transform life insurance into comprehensive protection vehicles addressing multiple risks through single policies

## Term Life Insurance Optimization

Term life insurance provides maximum death benefit for minimum cost, appropriate for most people during wealth accumulation years when protection needs are highest and cash flow is limited. A healthy 35-year-old can get $1 million in 20-year term coverage for $40-70 monthly. This protects dependents while you build wealth through other vehicles. Term insurance is pure protection without an investment component, you're buying peace of mind, not building assets.

The ladder strategy optimizes term insurance by staggering multiple policies with different terms:

- Instead of one $1 million 30-year policy, structure multiple policies
- Buy $500,000 for 30 years (covering entire mortgage period)
- Add $300,000 for 20 years (until kids graduate college)
- Include $200,000 for 10 years (covering peak earning years)
- As mortgages are paid and children become independent, coverage naturally decreases
- This strategy provides maximum coverage when needed while reducing costs over time

Conversion privileges transform term insurance into permanent coverage without new underwriting, providing valuable options as circumstances change:

- Most quality term policies allow converting to permanent insurance at the same health rating
- Someone diagnosed with cancer could convert term to whole life at original healthy rates
- This option has tremendous value, making convertible term superior to non-convertible
- Even at slightly higher cost, conversion privileges justify the premium

Return of premium (ROP) term insurance refunds all premiums if you outlive the term, combining protection with forced savings. Although costing 2-3 times more than standard term insurance, ROP provides psychological benefits for those who dislike "wasting" money on unused coverage. The returned premiums can fund retirement or be reinvested. However, the opportunity cost of higher premiums often makes standard terms plus separate investing superior mathematically.

## Tax Strategy Implementation

Life insurance tax advantages multiply when coordinated with overall financial planning. The modified endowment contract (MEC) rules limit premium payments to prevent policies from becoming pure investment vehicles. Understanding these limits enables maximum tax-advantaged funding without triggering MEC status, which would eliminate tax-free loan provisions. Proper structuring maintains life insurance tax benefits while maximizing investment components.

Premium financing strategies enable high-net-worth individuals to acquire large policies without massive cash outlays:

- Banks lend premiums at competitive rates, with policies as collateral
- Interest may be deductible if structured properly
- Death benefits repay loans with remainder to heirs
- This leverage amplifies estate values
- Can provide arbitrage opportunities when policy returns exceed loan costs
- Complexity and risk make premium financing appropriate only for sophisticated investors with substantial assets

The retirement income strategy uses life insurance to create tax-free retirement cash flow while preserving Social Security and Medicare benefits:

- Unlike IRA withdrawals that increase taxable income, life insurance loans don't count as income
- Access retirement funds without pushing Social Security into higher tax brackets
- Avoid triggering Medicare premium surcharges
- For high earners who've maximized other retirement accounts, provides additional tax-advantaged accumulation
- Distribution flexibility unavailable in traditional retirement accounts

Pension maximization strategies use life insurance to enable taking higher pension payouts while protecting spouses:

- Instead of accepting reduced joint-and-survivor pensions, retirees take maximum single-life payouts
- Buy life insurance protecting spouses with the difference
- If structured properly, provides more retirement income plus larger survivor benefits
- Can increase retirement income by 20-40% for healthy retirees
- Requires careful analysis but offers significant income enhancement

## Estate Planning Applications

Life insurance serves unique estate planning functions beyond simple wealth transfer. The instant estate creation aspect provides immediate wealth for young families who haven't had time to accumulate assets. A 30-year-old buying $2 million in term insurance creates instant estate value protecting family lifestyle regardless of accumulated savings. This leverages small premium payments into massive protection during vulnerable accumulation years.

Estate tax liquidity becomes critical for families with illiquid assets:

- **Business owners:** May face selling companies to pay estate taxes
- **Real estate investors:** Might liquidate properties at unfavorable prices
- **Art collectors:** Could be forced to auction collections quickly
- **Farm families:** Risk losing generational land to tax obligations
- Life insurance provides instant liquidity at precisely when needed, preventing forced asset sales

For estates facing 40% federal estate taxes plus state taxes, life insurance prevents wealth destruction from tax obligations.

The wealth replacement trust strategy enables charitable giving while preserving family inheritance:

- Donors give appreciated assets to charity,

receiving tax deductions and avoiding capital gains
- Life insurance replaces the donated value for heirs, often at pennies on the dollar
- Example: A 60-year-old donates $1 million in appreciated stock
- Receives $400,000 in tax benefits
- Buys $1 million in life insurance for $200,000
- Result: Charity receives $1 million, family receives $1 million, donor saves $200,000

Business succession planning relies heavily on life insurance:

- **Buy-sell agreements:** Funded with life insurance ensure smooth ownership transition when partners die
- **Key person insurance:** Protects against revenue loss from essential employee deaths
- **Business loan protection:** Ensures loans are repaid if owner dies
- **Employee retention:** Golden handcuff plans using life insurance
- These applications preserve business value and enable continuation during vulnerable transition periods

Without proper life insurance planning, businesses often fail when owners or key employees die unexpectedly.

## Chapter 9 Quick Wins:

Evaluate Existing Coverage Gaps - List current coverage:

Employer life insurance $,

*Personal term $,*

Whole/UL $.

*Total:* $. Compared to the need calculated above.

Gap: $____. Write three actions to close this gap with deadlines.

**10**

---

## ADVANCED WEALTH STRATEGIES

Tax optimization represents the highest return, lowest risk advanced strategy available to wealth builders. The difference between tax-efficient and tax-inefficient investing can be 30% or more of total returns over time. Every dollar saved in taxes compounds just like investment returns.

## The Mathematics Are Staggering:

Two investors each earning 10% annual returns on $100,000 investments:

- **Tax-inefficient investor** (paying 35% on gains annually): $432,000 after 30 years
- **Tax-efficient investor** (deferring taxes until the end): $1,744,940, then after paying taxes on gains, keeps $1,284,000

The difference of $852,000 comes purely from tax strategy, not superior investment selection.

## Tax-Advantage Accounts: The Foundation

Maximize these accounts before taxable investing:

- **401(k) plans:** Pre-tax contributions reducing current taxable income
- **Traditional IRAs:** Tax-deductible contributions with tax-deferred growth
- **Roth IRAs:** After-tax contributions with tax-free growth and withdrawals
- **HSAs:** Triple tax advantage, deductible, tax-free growth, tax-free medical withdrawals
- **529 Plans:** Tax-free growth and withdrawals for education expenses

## The Hierarchy of Account Funding:

1 Contribute enough to 401(k) to capture full employer match (immediate 50-100% return)

2 Max out HSA contributions for triple tax advantages

3 Contribute to Roth IRA if eligible, or backdoor Roth if above income limits

4 Max remaining 401(k) space

5 Consider 529 plans for education funding

6 Only after exhausting tax-advantaged accounts should taxable accounts receive investment dollars

**Asset Location Strategy:** Hold tax-inefficient investments (bonds, REITs, high-dividend stocks) in tax-advantaged accounts. Place tax-efficient investments (index funds, growth stocks) in taxable accounts. This strategic placement can add 0.5-1% to annual after-tax returns.

## The Roth Conversion Ladder

Enables early retirement by providing penalty-free access to retirement funds before age 59½. Convert traditional IRA funds to Roth IRA, pay taxes on conversions at potentially lower rates, then access the converted principal penalty-free after five years.

**The Mechanics:**

• Each year, convert exactly enough traditional IRA funds to fill up lower tax brackets

• After five years, the first conversion's principal becomes accessible penalty-free

• By year six, you have both year one's principal available and year six's conversion processing

• Creates sustainable income flow for early retirement

**Tax bracket arbitrage:** If you contribute to traditional accounts while in the 32% bracket but convert while in the 12% bracket, you save 20% on every dollar.

## Tax Loss Harvesting Mastery

Transform market volatility into tax savings by systematically realizing losses to offset gains and up to $3,000 of ordinary income annually. Excess losses carry forward indefinitely.

**Avoiding Wash Sale Rules:**

• Selling an S&P 500 ETF and buying a different S&P 500 ETF triggers wash sales

• Selling an S&P 500 fund and buying a total market fund preserves tax losses

• Individual stocks of different companies in same sector maintain similar exposure

**Direct indexing** supercharges this by allowing ownership of individual stocks rather than funds. In volatile markets, this can generate tax losses equal to 20-30% of portfolio value in the first year, adding 1-2% to annual after-tax returns.

## Estate Planning Architecture

Proper structure can eliminate estate taxes, protect assets from creditors, and ensure your wealth furthers your values long after death.

**Revocable Living Trusts (The Foundation):**
- Probate avoidance: Skip the public, expensive court process
- Privacy protection: Assets transfer privately without public records
- Cost savings: Avoid 3-7% probate costs on estate value
- Speed: Immediate transfer versus 6-18 months probate process

**Advanced Structures:**
- **Irrevocable Life Insurance Trust (ILIT):** Holds life insurance outside your estate, preventing 40% estate tax on death benefits
- **Charitable Remainder Trusts:** Provide income during life while generating immediate tax deductions
- **Generation-Skipping Trusts:** Preserve wealth across multiple generations by avoiding estate taxes at each generational transfer

**Annual Gift Tax Exclusion:**
- Transfer $17,000 per recipient tax-free yearly ($34,000 for couples)
- Fund 529 education accounts with five years upfront, $85,000 immediately

- Move hundreds of thousands from taxable estates annually

## Asset Protection Fortification

In a society where 15 million lawsuits are filed annually, proper protection is essential. The key is implementing protection before problems arise, attempting to shield assets after claims emerge constitutes fraudulent transfer.

## $3 Million Lawsuit That Never Touched Them

Dr. Rachel Chen had just finished her residency when she met attorney James Morrison at a financial planning seminar. While other young doctors were buying Teslas, Rachel was there learning about something called "asset protection."

"You're paranoid," her colleague Dr. Kevin Park laughed when Rachel spent $5,000 setting up LLCs and trusts. "We have malpractice insurance." Kevin used that $5,000 for a vacation to Bali instead.

Rachel's structure seemed excessive to everyone:

- Each rental property in its own LLC
- A Nevada Asset Protection Trust for her investment accounts
- Maximizing ERISA-protected 401(k) contributions
- A $5 million umbrella insurance policy for $500/year
- Her home titled to an irrevocable trust with her as beneficiary

"Why so complicated?" Kevin asked, investing everything in a joint account with his wife.

Five years later, they both faced nightmares on the same day.

Kevin's patient sued for $8 million after a surgery complication. His malpractice insurance covered $3 million. The remaining $5 million? That was on Kevin. Within months, liens appeared on his house, his investment accounts were frozen, and his wife's inheritance was at risk because everything was jointly owned.

Rachel's tenant fell through a railing, suing for $4 million. But here's what happened:

- The LLC owning that property was the only entity named in the suit
- Her other properties remained untouched
- Her personal assets were invisible behind the trust walls
- The umbrella policy kicked in up to $5 million
- Her retirement accounts were federally protected

The case settled for $2 million, paid entirely by insurance.

But the story's real twist came during the lawsuits.

Kevin's attorney delivered the bad news: "Everything titled in your name is at risk. The joint accounts, the house, even your future earnings can be garnished."

Rachel's attorney had different news: "They can't touch anything beyond that single LLC and what insurance covers. Your trusts were established four years ago, well past the challenge period."

**The aftermath revealed the true cost of protection:**
Kevin's losses:

- $5 million personal judgment
- Home sold in forced sale
- Investment accounts liquidated
- 25% of wages garnished for 10 years

**Total wealth destroyed: $3.2 million**

. . .

Rachel's losses:

- $0 personal assets touched
- Insurance deductible: $10,000
- Legal fees: $15,000

**Total cost: $25,000**

"But wait," Kevin protested when they met for coffee after everything settled. "You spent so much on all those structures."

Rachel pulled up her phone calculator. "Over five years, I spent $20,000 on LLCs, trusts, and legal fees. You lost $3.2 million. My protection cost 0.6% of what you lost."

She showed him something else, her estate plan. The generation-skipping trusts, the ILITs holding life insurance outside her taxable estate, the charitable remainder trust generating income while providing massive tax deductions.

"This isn't just about protection from lawsuits," she explained. "My kids will inherit $10 million tax-free. Yours would have paid $4 million in estate taxes, if there was anything left."

Kevin started over at 38, finally understanding what Rachel knew at 28: You don't buy insurance because you expect your house to burn down. You build financial fortresses because one lawsuit, one accident, one unexpected event shouldn't destroy decades of wealth building.

Rachel's final words haunted him: "The time to build an ark isn't when it starts raining. It's when the sky is clear and everyone thinks you're crazy for gathering wood."

Today, Kevin tells every young doctor he meets: "Spend the $5,000. Set up the structures. Be paranoid. Because the difference between protected and exposed isn't measured in thousands, it's measured in millions."

## Asset Protection Strategies

**Liability Insurance (First Defense Layer):**
- $5 million umbrella policy costs ~$500 annually
- Exceptional value for catastrophic protection
- For professionals: Add errors and omissions or malpractice insurance

**Limited Liability Companies (LLCs):**
- Rental properties isolated in separate LLCs limit liability to individual properties
- Business operations conducted through LLCs protect personal wealth
- Maintain corporate formalities: separate accounts, proper documentation, arm's length transactions

**Domestic Asset Protection Trusts:**
- Available in Nevada, Delaware, and Alaska
- Protect assets from future creditors while allowing discretionary distributions
- After statutory periods (2-4 years), assets become largely untouchable by creditors

**Retirement Account Protection:**
- ERISA-qualified plans (401(k)s): Unlimited federal bankruptcy protection
- IRAs: Protection up to $1.5 million in bankruptcy
- Many states provide additional unlimited protection outside bankruptcy

## Alternative Investment

**Real Estate Syndications:**
- Target 15-20% annual returns through income and appreciation

• Depreciation passes through creating paper losses offsetting other income

• Completely passive while receiving active tax benefits

**Private Equity and Venture Capital:**

• Potential for 10-100x returns by investing in private companies

• Highly risky and illiquid, diversification crucial

• Power law distribution: One successful investment can offset numerous failures

**Cryptocurrency and Digital Assets:**

• Proper position sizing: 5-10% of portfolios provides asymmetric upside while limiting downside

• Understand tax implications around staking rewards and DeFi transactions

**Commodities and Precious Metals:**

• Inflation hedging and portfolio diversification uncorrelated with traditional assets

• Physical gold and silver offer disaster insurance and currency debasement protection

## Business Equity Opimization

Building business equity creates wealth multiples beyond employment income through ownership of productive assets.

**Business Valuation Multiples:**

• Software companies: 5-10x revenue multiples

• Service businesses: 1-3x revenue multiples

• Manufacturing: 3-6x EBITDA

• E-commerce: 2-4x revenue depending on margins

• Subscription businesses: 3-7x recurring revenue

A business generating $1 million in revenue worth 5x

creates $5 million in wealth, impossible through employment savings.

**Systematic Value Building:**

• Recurring revenue models command premium valuations

• Diversified customer bases reduce risk and increase value

• Documented systems and processes enable scalability

• Strong management teams reduce owner dependence

• Each improvement might increase valuation multiples by 0.5-1x

## Leverage Strategies For Wealth

**Real Estate Leverage (Most Accessible):** Buying a $500,000 property with $100,000 down and earning 5% appreciation generates 25% return on invested capital, 5x unleveraged returns.

**Margin Investing (Requires Extreme Caution):**

• Limit borrowing to 20-30% of portfolio value maximum

• Maintain substantial cash reserves for margin calls

• Avoid margin during volatile market periods

• Understand forced liquidation risks

**Business Leverage:**

• Equipment financing, working capital lines, and expansion loans enable faster scaling

• Key: Match debt terms to asset lives and revenue generation

• Conservative leverage ratios maintaining 2x or higher debt service coverage

**Options Strategies:**

• Long-term equity anticipation securities (LEAPS)

enable controlling stock positions for fractions of purchase prices

- Selling covered calls generates income from existing positions
- Credit spreads profit from time decay with defined risk

## Advanced Tax Strategies

**Conservation Easements:**

- Massive tax deductions for preserving land while maintaining ownership and use
- Donating development rights generates deductions often exceeding property value
- Can eliminate entire years of tax liability

**Opportunity Zone Investments (Triple Tax Benefits):**

- Defer capital gains taxes by reinvesting within 180 days
- Reduce taxable gain amount through basis step-ups
- Eliminate all appreciation taxes after 10-year holding period

**Charitable Strategies:**

- Donor-advised funds enable immediate deductions while controlling donation timing
- Charitable remainder trusts provide lifetime income, immediate deductions, and estate tax reduction
- Donating appreciated assets avoids capital gains while receiving full value deductions

**Cost Segregation Studies (For Real Estate):**

- Accelerate depreciation deductions by identifying components depreciable over 5, 7, or 15 years instead of 27.5 or 39 years
- Can create first-year losses exceeding down payments
- For real estate professionals, these losses offset ordinary income

## International Wealth Strategies

**Offshore Banking Benefits:**
- Asset protection through jurisdictional diversification
- Currency diversification protecting against dollar devaluation
- Privacy protection within legal reporting requirements
- Countries like Singapore, Switzerland offer stable banking with strong privacy laws

**Digital Nomad Strategies:**
- Earn developed country incomes while living in lower-cost locations
- Foreign earned income exclusion and strategic residency planning can eliminate or reduce tax burdens
- Can accelerate wealth accumulation by 3-5x through expense reduction and tax optimization

Understanding and implementing these advanced strategies transforms good investors into wealthy investors through the power of keeping more of what you earn. The mathematics of tax efficiency, asset protection, and strategic leverage compound over decades to create extraordinary wealth differences.

## Chapter 10 Quick Wins:

**Complete Your Advanced Tax Strategy Scorecard** - Rate yourself 1-10 on each strategy:

- Tax-advantaged account maximization: ___/10
- Asset location optimization: ___/10
- Tax loss harvesting: ___/10
- Estate planning: ___/10
- Asset protection: ___/10

- Alternative investments: ___/10
- Business equity building: ___/10
- Strategic leverage use: ___/10
- International diversification: ___/10

Total: ___/90. Any item under 5 needs immediate attention. Write your three lowest scores and one specific action for each with a completion date.

## 11

## GENERATIONAL
## WEALTH ARCHITECTURE

Generational wealth transcends individual financial success, creating prosperity that compounds across decades and centuries. The difference between temporary affluence and a lasting dynasty lies not in the amount of wealth created but in the systems designed to preserve, grow, and transfer it across generations. While 70% of wealthy families lose their wealth by the second generation and 90% by the third, families who understand generational wealth principles create legacies lasting centuries.

The generational wealth equation operates on three dimensions simultaneously: wealth creation, wealth preservation, and wealth transfer. Creation without preservation leads to dissipation through lifestyle inflation, poor investments, or economic downturns. Preservation without transfer results in estate taxes, family conflicts, or lost opportunities consuming accumulated assets. Transfer without proper structure creates entitled heirs who destroy what previous generations built. Success requires orchestrating all three dimensions through deliberate architecture.

The mathematical power of multi-generational compounding dwarfs single-lifetime accumulation. A family investing $100,000 at 8% annual returns sees it grow to $2.2 million over 40 years, impressive single-generation wealth. But maintaining that discipline across three generations transforms $100,000 into $47 million over 120 years. This exponential growth explains how families like the Rothschilds, Rockefellers, and Waltons built wealth measured in hundreds of billions. They understood that time, not amount, determines ultimate wealth.

## Building a Lasting Dynasty

While 70% of wealthy families lose their wealth by the second generation and 90% by the third, families who understand generational wealth principles create legacies lasting centuries.

**The Three Dimensions (All Required):**
- **Wealth Creation:** Building substantial assets
- **Wealth Preservation:** Protecting from lifestyle inflation, poor investments, or economic downturns
- **Wealth Transfer:** Proper structure preventing estate taxes, family conflicts, or entitled heirs

**The Mathematical Power:**
A family investing $100,000 at 8% annual returns:
- Single generation (40 years): $2.2 million
- Three generations (120 years): $47 million

**Time, not amount, determines ultimate wealth.**

**The Compound Effect Beyond Money:**
- **Intellectual capital:** Education, skills, wisdom
- **Social capital:** Networks, reputation, relationships
- **Cultural capital:** Values, habits, traditions
- **Human capital:** Health, capabilities

• **Spiritual capital:** Purpose, meaning, family mission

## The Tale Of Two Neighbors

Two families on the same street each sold their businesses for $10 million in the same year. Three generations later, their descendants' lives couldn't be more different.

The Thompsons celebrated with luxury, a mansion, exotic vacations, and the promise that their children would never struggle. They paid for everything: homes, weddings, college tuitions. Their philosophy was simple: "We worked hard so our kids won't have to."

By the third generation, the family trust held less than $500,000. Family gatherings became tense battles over a dwindling pie.

The Johnsons kept their modest home and created the "Family Learning Fund." They matched dollars their children earned, funded business ventures that required business plans, and lent rather than gave. Sunday dinners included investment discussions. Children attended annual "Family Board Meetings," presenting reports on their small investment accounts. Each grandchild worked summers in the family business, learning from the ground up.

Seventy-five years later, the Johnson family's wealth had grown to $150 million. More importantly, it had produced two doctors, three entrepreneurs, and several successful executives, each capable of creating wealth independently. Their gatherings centered around new ventures and teaching the youngest generation.

The difference wasn't luck, it was philosophy.

The Thompsons used wealth to eliminate struggle, inadvertently eliminating growth. The Johnsons used wealth to amplify opportunity while maintaining the challenges that build character.

The question every wealth-building family must answer isn't "How much can we give?" but "How can we develop capable children?"

## Building The Financial Foundation

**The 100-Year Portfolio:** Maintain equity-heavy allocations knowing short-term volatility becomes irrelevant across century timespans. A portfolio suffering 50% drawdowns but averaging 12% returns vastly outperforms stable 6% returns over multiple generations.

**Asset Class Diversification (no single class exceeds 40%):**
- Real estate: Inflation protection and income
- Equities: Growth potential and liquidity
- Private businesses: Cash flow and tax advantages
- Precious metals: Currency debasement hedge
- Intellectual property: Recurring royalties
- Art and collectibles: Value storage

**Geographic Diversification:** Three-flag theory, live in one country, maintain businesses in another, keep investments in a third.

**The Perpetual Wealth Machine:** If a family spends $500,000 annually and investments yield 5%, they need $10 million to maintain lifestyle without depleting principal. Target $20 million for margin.

## Family Financial Education

**Age-Appropriate Education:**

- **Ages 3-5:** Money basics, earning through chores, saving
- **Ages 6-10:** Managing allowances, understanding prices, needs vs. wants
- **Ages 11-14:** Bank accounts, compound interest, basic investing
- **Ages 15-18:** Stock market participation, business fundamentals, tax basics
- **Ages 19-25:** Advanced investing, estate planning, wealth management

**The Family Bank:** Lend money at market rates with formal agreements. Require business plans for larger amounts. This teaches that money has cost and loans require repayment.

**Entrepreneurship Education:** Match their business investments dollar-for-dollar. Celebrate failures as learning experiences.

**Investment Participation:** Give children small investment accounts. Include teenagers in investment meetings. This creates sophisticated investors rather than vulnerable beneficiaries.

## Trust Architecture

**Dynasty Trusts:** Perpetuate wealth indefinitely by avoiding estate taxes at each generational transfer. Assets benefit unlimited generations without triggering transfer taxes. The Rockefeller trusts, established over a century ago, still provide for descendants today.

IRREVOCABLE TRUST OPTIONS:

- **SLAT**: Indirect benefit access through spouse
- **Charitable Lead Trust**: Income to charity, remainder to heirs
- **GRAT**: Transfer appreciation tax-free
- **QPRT**: Transfer homes at discounted values

**Distribution Strategies:**

- **Discretionary trusts**: Distribute based on beneficiary maturity
- **Incentive trusts**: Tie distributions to achievements
- **Staggered distributions**: Prevent single poor decisions from destroying inheritance

## Family Governance

**The Family Constitution:** Documents shared values, vision, and principles. Articulates why wealth exists, how it should be used, and what behaviors are expected. Becomes the North Star when founders are gone.

**Family Councils:** Regular meetings to discuss investments, philanthropy, and family business. Younger generations observe before gaining voting rights. Written agendas and resolutions create accountability.

**The Family Office:**

- Investment management
- Tax planning and compliance
- Estate planning and trust administration
- Family services and property management
- Philanthropy and foundation management

**Next Generation Preparation:** Internships in family businesses, board observer positions, investment committee participation, leadership development, mentorship programs.

## Tax Optimization Across Generations

**Estate Tax Exemption:** Current exemptions of $13 million per person ($26 million for couples) won't last forever. Using exemptions now locks in current benefits. Use it or lose it.

**GRATs:** Mark Zuckerberg reportedly transferred $37 million to heirs tax-free through GRATs before Facebook's IPO.

**CLATs:** The Jackie Onassis trust transferred $100 million to heirs after paying charity, avoiding tens of millions in estate taxes.

**Generation-Skipping Tax Planning:**
- Utilize GST exemptions matching estate tax exemptions
- Structure dynasty trusts to avoid GST tax forever
- Make direct gifts to grandchildren using annual exclusions


## Family Enterprises

**Governance (Separate Family from Business):**
- Family employment requires legitimate qualifications
- Compensation matches market rates
- Performance standards apply equally
- Outside directors provide oversight
- Professional management systems

**Ownership Transition:**
- Voting shares with family leaders
- Non-voting shares distribute economic benefits
- Buy-sell agreements establish valuation methods
- Stock option plans incentivize key employees

## Philanthropy And Legacy

**Family Foundations:** Create shared family purpose beyond wealth preservation. Children learn social responsibility through participation. Family bonds strengthen through collective impact.

**Donor-Advised Funds:** Simpler alternatives providing immediate tax deductions, capital gains avoidance, and strategic giving timing.

**Impact Investing:** Align investments with values while generating returns. Engages younger generations who demand purpose alongside profit.

**Legacy Beyond Financial Assets:**
- **Ethical wills:** Communicate values and life lessons
- **Family histories:** Preserve stories providing identity
- **Video messages:** Create personal connections across time
- **Wisdom journals:** Document lessons for descendants


## Protecting Wealth

**Prenuptial Agreements:** Protect pre-marital assets, inheritances, and family business interests. Prevent single divorces from destroying multi-generational wealth.

**Asset Protection Trusts:**
- **Domestic** (Nevada, Delaware): Strong protection, US jurisdiction
- **Offshore** (Cook Islands, Nevis): Stronger protection for international structures
- Multiple trust layers create defense in depth

**Addiction and Mental Health Protocols:**
- Intervention procedures and treatment funding

- Trust provisions suspend distributions during active addiction
- Professional trustees override family emotions
- Treatment funding separate from inheritance

**Professional Advisory Teams:**

- Wealth psychologists: Address family dynamics
- Investment advisors: Manage portfolios institutionally
- Estate attorneys: Maintain legal structures
- Tax advisors: Optimize strategies across generations
- Family business consultants: Ensure operational excellence

Generational wealth isn't about giving children everything, it's about developing capable children who can create their own wealth while stewarding what's been built. Success requires orchestrating creation, preservation, and transfer through deliberate architecture, education, governance, and protection systems that compound advantages across unlimited generations.

## Chapter 11 Quick Wins:

Create Your Trust Structure Blueprint - Draw your current assets at the top of a page. Below, draw boxes for potential trusts:

- Revocable Living Trust (probate avoidance)
- Dynasty Trust (multi-generational)
- Charitable Trust (tax deduction) Draw arrows showing which assets would flow to which trusts. Write the benefits next to each trust. Circle the one you'll establish first.

## 12

## CONCLUSION

Throughout this book, we've dismantled the mythology surrounding wealth and replaced it with mathematical certainty. The equation for financial freedom isn't mysterious, it's a systematic formula that works regardless of starting point, education level, or current circumstances. The components are now clear: eliminate debt to stop negative compound interest, save systematically to create investment capital, invest wisely to harness positive compound returns, optimize taxes to keep more of what you earn, build businesses to multiply income, acquire real estate for multiple return streams, and ultimately construct systems that perpetuate wealth across generations.

Each chapter has provided a piece of the wealth-building puzzle, and now it's time to see the complete picture. The foundation begins with understanding money's true nature, that it represents stored energy, and that it can be put to work independently of human labour.This understanding transforms your relationship with money from scarcity-based hoarding to abundance-based multiplication.

When you grasp that money can work harder and longer than any human, generating returns 24/7/365, you stop trading time for money and start making money work for you.

The mathematical progression from debt slave to financial sovereign follows predictable stages. First, you eliminate high-interest debt that creates negative compound spirals, freeing cash flow for wealth building. Next, you optimize banking and savings to maximize returns on emergency funds and operational capital. Then you begin investing systematically in index funds and tax-advantaged accounts, letting compound interest work its exponential magic. As capital accumulates, you diversify into real estate, business ventures, and alternative investments, creating multiple uncorrelated return streams. Finally, you implement advanced strategies, tax optimization, estate planning, asset protection, that preserve and perpetuate wealth indefinitely.

This progression isn't theoretical but mathematical certainty. A 25-year-old who eliminates debt, saves 20% of income, invests in index funds returning 10% annually, and follows the strategies outlined in this book will accumulate over $3 million by age 65 from a $50,000 salary. Add side hustles increasing income by 30%, real estate providing 20% returns through leverage, and business equity worth 5x annual revenue, and that same person can achieve financial independence by age 45 with $5-10 million in net worth. These aren't fantasies but mathematical outcomes of applying the principles consistently.

## The Compound Effect of Combined Strategies

The true power of this system emerges when strategies compound upon each other. Debt elimination doesn't just save interest, it frees cash flow that accelerates investment accumulation. Tax optimization doesn't just reduce current taxes, it increases investable capital that compounds for decades. Side hustles don't just provide extra income, they can evolve into scalable businesses worth millions. Each strategy amplifies the others, creating exponential rather than linear wealth growth.

Consider how the strategies interconnect and reinforce each other. High-yield savings optimization might seem trivial, earning 5% instead of 0.01% on emergency funds. But that extra $500 annual return on a $10,000 emergency fund, invested over 30 years, becomes $57,000. That $57,000 could fund a real estate down payment, generating $200,000 in appreciation over a decade. That appreciation could fund a business venture, creating a company worth $2 million. Each small optimization cascades into massive wealth differences over time.

The synergy between earned income and investment income creates particular power. Your job provides the seed capital for investments. Investments generate passive income that reduces dependence on employment. This reduced dependence enables taking calculated risks, starting businesses, making aggressive investments, pursuing opportunities, that employed individuals depending on paychecks cannot afford. Eventually, investment income exceeds living expenses, making employment optional. This is the mathematical crossover point where you achieve true financial freedom.

The tax advantages of combining strategies multiply wealth accumulation dramatically. Business ownership enables deducting expenses that employees cannot. Real estate provides depreciation shields offsetting other income. Retirement accounts defer or eliminate taxes on investment growth. Life insurance provides tax-free accumulation and distribution. When strategically combined, these tax advantages can reduce lifetime tax burden by millions, effectively doubling or tripling after-tax wealth accumulation compared to naive tax planning.

## The Modern Acceleration Factors

Today's wealth builders possess advantages previous generations couldn't imagine. Digital technology has democratized access to investments, education, and global markets. You can invest in index funds with $1, start global businesses from your bedroom, access world-class education free online, and reach billions of customers through the internet. These tools compress wealth-building timelines from generations to decades or even years for those who understand and utilize them.

The cryptocurrency revolution, particularly Bitcoin, represents a once-in-a-generation wealth transfer opportunity. While speculative and volatile, the mathematical case for Bitcoin achieving $1 million or higher is compelling given its fixed supply, growing adoption, and superior monetary properties compared to fiat currencies being debased globally. A small allocation to Bitcoin, perhaps 5-10% of portfolio, provides asymmetric upside with limited downside. Those who understand this opportunity and act while Bitcoin remains below $100,000 may build generational wealth from modest investments.

The gig economy and remote work have fundamentally altered income generation possibilities. Geographic arbitrage, earning San Francisco salaries while living in Kansas, can triple effective income. Multiple income streams through freelancing, consulting, and digital products can double or triple base salaries. Online businesses can scale globally without physical infrastructure. These opportunities didn't exist twenty years ago but now enable ordinary people to generate extraordinary income.

Artificial intelligence and automation are creating unprecedented leverage opportunities. AI tools can multiply productivity 10x in writing, coding, design, and analysis. Automation platforms can run entire businesses with minimal human involvement. Smart contracts can execute complex financial transactions automatically. Those who embrace these technologies rather than fear them will capture disproportionate wealth as productivity advantages compound over time.

## The Mindset Revolution Required

Building wealth requires more than understanding mathematics, it demands a fundamental mindset transformation. The poverty mindset sees money as scarce, savings as sacrifice, and wealth as unattainable. The wealth mindset sees money as abundant, savings as purchasing future freedom, and wealth as mathematical inevitability given proper strategies and time. This shift from scarcity to abundance thinking changes every financial decision.

The employee mindset must evolve into the owner mindset. Employees think in terms of hourly wages and annual salaries. Owners think in terms of equity value and business multiples. Employees trade time for money linearly. Owners build systems generating money independently of time. Employees see businesses as employers. Owners see businesses as wealth-creation vehicles. This transformation from employee to owner thinking is essential for building substantial wealth.

The consumer mindset must transform into the investor mindset. Consumers see money as something to spend on immediate pleasures. Investors see money as seeds to plant for future harvests. Consumers evaluate purchases based on affordability. Investors evaluate purchases based on opportunity cost, what investment returns are foregone. Consumers accumulate depreciating liabilities. Investors accumulate appreciating assets. This shift from consumption to investment changes wealth trajectories dramatically.

The short-term mindset must extend to long-term thinking. Most people plan days or weeks ahead. Wealth builders plan decades ahead. Short-term thinking leads to decisions optimizing immediate pleasure at future expense. Long-term thinking leads to decisions accepting temporary sacrifice for permanent prosperity. The ability to delay gratification and think in decade-long timeframes separates the wealthy from everyone else.

## The Implementation Roadmap

Knowledge without action remains merely potential. The difference between those who build wealth and those who simply read about it is implementation. The roadmap from your current situation to financial freedom follows a clear sequence, though the timeline varies based on starting point and intensity of application.

Phase One (Months 1-6): Foundation Building. Eliminate all high-interest debt using avalanche or snowball methods. Build a $1,000-2,500 starter emergency fund. Open high-yield savings accounts earning 5% instead of 0.01%. Start investing $100 monthly in index funds automatically. Begin tracking expenses and creating budgets. Read one financial book monthly. Calculate net worth and track monthly.

These foundational actions stop the bleeding and begin forward momentum.

Phase Two (Months 7-24): Acceleration. Increase income through raises, job changes, or side hustles by 20-50%. Build a full 3-6 month emergency fund in high-yield savings. Max out employer 401(k) match and open Roth IRA. Increase investment rate to 15-20% of gross income. Start a side business generating $500-2,000 monthly. Optimize all spending categories for maximum value. Learn basic tax strategies and implement them. These acceleration activities multiply wealth-building velocity.

Phase Three (Years 2-5): Expansion. Scale side business to $5,000+ monthly or sellable assets. Purchase first rental property using house hacking or traditional investing. Max out all tax-advantaged retirement accounts. Build a taxable investment portfolio for flexibility. Implement advanced tax strategies like tax loss harvesting. Create basic estate planning documents. Build business credit separate from personal credit. These expansion activities create multiple wealth engines.

Phase Four (Years 5-10): Optimization. Build a real estate portfolio to 5-10 units generating passive income. Scale business to $1 million+ revenue or exit for 3-5x multiple. Achieve investment portfolio equal to 10x annual expenses. Implement sophisticated tax strategies reducing lifetime burden by millions. Create a comprehensive estate plan with trusts and asset protection. Develop multiple uncorrelated income streams. These optimization activities create true financial independence.

Phase Five (Years 10+): Perpetuation. Focus on wealth preservation and transfer strategies. Build family governance structures and education systems. Create charitable giving strategies aligning with values. Implement generational wealth preservation trusts. Develop successor leadership in businesses. Focus on impact and legacy beyond money. These perpetuation activities ensure wealth benefits multiple generations.

## The Obstacles You'll Face

The path to wealth isn't smooth or easy, if it were, everyone would be wealthy. Understanding the obstacles you'll encounter and preparing strategies to overcome them increases success probability dramatically. These challenges are predictable and surmountable with proper preparation and mindset.

Social pressure will be your first and most persistent obstacle. Friends and family won't understand why you're saving instead of spending, investing instead of consuming, building instead of relaxing. They'll question your choices, mock your discipline, and tempt you toward their lifestyle. The solution is finding like-minded communities, online forums, local investment clubs, entrepreneurship groups, that support rather than sabotage your wealth-building journey.

Market volatility will test your resolve repeatedly. Your investments will decline 20%, 30%, even 50% during your wealth-building journey. These declines are temporary, but the fear they generate is real and powerful. The solution is understanding market history, every crash has been followed by recovery and new highs. Automate investments to continue during downturns. View crashes as opportunities to buy assets on sale rather than reasons to sell in panic.

Lifestyle inflation will constantly tempt you to increase spending as income rises. Every raise, bonus, and windfall creates pressure to upgrade lifestyle rather than accelerate wealth building. The solution is automating savings increases before lifestyle has a chance to adjust. When income increases, immediately redirect 50% or more to investments before growing accustomed to the additional cash flow.

Complexity paralysis will strike as strategies become more sophisticated. Tax optimization, estate planning, business structure, and international diversification can seem overwhelming. The solution is implementing strategies incrementally rather than simultaneously. Master basic investing before attempting real estate. Understand domestic markets before going international. Build simple businesses before complex structures. Progress step by step rather than attempting everything immediately.

## The Price of Inaction

While this book has focused on the rewards of building wealth, it's equally important to understand the devastating cost of inaction. Every day you delay implementing these strategies costs exponentially more than you realize. The price of procrastination isn't linear but exponential due to compound interest working against you.

Consider the mathematics of delay. A 25-year-old investing $500 monthly at 10% returns accumulates $3.16 million by 65. Starting at 35 accumulates only $1.13 million. That ten-year delay costs $2 million, a 64% reduction in final wealth. Starting at 45 accumulates only $380,000. That twenty-year delay costs $2.78 million, an 88% reduction. Every year of delay doesn't just postpone wealth, it permanently destroys it.

The opportunity cost extends beyond just investment returns. Debt continues accumulating interest while you procrastinate about elimination. Inflation continues eroding purchasing power while you leave money in checking accounts. Taxes continue consuming income while you ignore optimization strategies. Rent continues enriching landlords while you delay real estate investment. Every day of inaction transfers wealth from your future to others' presents.

The generational impact of inaction is even more severe. Your children inherit not just your wealth but your financial habits and knowledge. If you don't build wealth, they start from zero. If you don't understand investing, neither will they. If you don't create businesses, they won't learn entrepreneurship. The cost of your inaction compounds across generations, potentially condemning your descendants to permanent wage slavery.

The psychological cost of inaction may be the highest price. Financial stress is the leading cause of divorce, depression, and health problems. Living paycheck to paycheck creates chronic anxiety that impairs decision-making and life enjoyment. Depending on employment for survival creates constant insecurity. Not having options limits life to mere survival rather than thriving. The price of not building wealth isn't just monetary, it's measured in stress, limitation, and unfulfilled potential.

## Your Wealth-Building Commitment

The time for learning has ended; the time for action has arrived. You now possess the complete blueprint for building wealth, the principles, strategies, and tactics that transform ordinary earners into millionaires and beyond. The only remaining variable is your commitment to implementation. Will you be among the few who apply this knowledge to transform their financial destiny, or among the many who read, nod, and continue their current path toward financial mediocrity?

Success requires making a formal commitment to yourself and your future. Write a contract with yourself specifying exactly what you'll accomplish in the next 30 days, 90 days, and one year. Include specific actions: opening investment accounts, eliminating specific debts, starting particular side hustles, implementing defined strategies. Sign this contract, date it, and place it where you'll see it daily. Share it with an accountability partner who will hold you to your commitments.

The compound effect of small actions creates enormous results over time. Opening a high-yield savings account takes ten minutes but generates thousands in additional interest over decades. Setting up automatic investing takes five minutes but builds millions over a lifetime. Starting a side hustle takes a weekend but can evolve into million-dollar businesses. Each small action you take today echoes across your entire financial future.

Remember that wealth building is a marathon, not a sprint. You'll face setbacks, make mistakes, and sometimes feel like giving up. Markets will crash, businesses will fail, investments will disappoint. These temporary defeats are learning opportunities, not reasons to quit. Every wealthy person has faced similar challenges. The difference is they persisted while others surrendered. Your commitment must extend beyond enthusiasm to discipline, beyond motivation to habit, beyond interest to obsession.

## The Legacy You'll Create

Building wealth transcends personal benefit to create ripples affecting countless lives across multiple generations. The wealth you build provides security for your family, opportunities for your children, and resources for causes you support. But beyond direct beneficiaries, your wealth-building journey inspires others to transform their own financial futures. You become living proof that ordinary people can achieve extraordinary financial results through discipline and proper strategies.

The knowledge and habits you develop while building wealth become family assets more valuable than money itself. Your children learn by observation that wealth is achievable through systematic effort rather than luck or inheritance. They absorb investment principles, business acumen, and financial discipline through daily exposure rather than formal education. These lessons, transmitted across generations, create financial dynasties from humble beginnings.

The businesses you build create employment, provide valuable services, and contribute to economic growth. The real estate you develop provides housing while building communities. The investments you make fund innovation and progress. The taxes you pay support social infrastructure. The charity you are eventually able to provide helps to address social challenges. Wealth building, properly pursued, benefits society broadly rather than just the individual.

The ultimate legacy isn't measured in dollars but in lives transformed. The employees who learn from your leadership. The customers served by your businesses. The causes advanced by your philanthropy. The family members provided opportunity and security. The readers inspired by your example to begin their own wealth-building journeys. This is the true measure of wealth, not what you accumulate but what you contribute.

## Your Journey Begins Now

The path from financial struggle to financial freedom stretches before you, clearly marked by the principles and strategies outlined in this book. You've learned that money follows mathematical principles as predictable as physics. You understand that wealth building is a systematic process, not a mysterious lottery. You possess the complete blueprint for transforming your financial future regardless of current circumstances.

The choice you face is simple but profound: Will you close this book and return to the same financial patterns that brought you here, or will you take the first concrete step toward the wealthy future you deserve? Will you continue accepting the limitations of paycheck-to-paycheck existence, or will you implement the strategies that guarantee financial transformation? Will you remain among the 95% who retire dependent on others, or join the 5% who achieve true financial independence?

Your financial transformation doesn't require perfection, only progression. You don't need to implement every strategy immediately, only begin with one. You don't need massive capital to start, only the commitment to begin where you are with what you have. Every millionaire started with their first dollar saved. Every real estate empire started with the first property. Every successful business started with the first customer. Your wealth-building journey starts with the first action you take after closing this book.

The mathematics are irrefutable. The strategies are proven. The tools are available. The opportunities are abundant. The only variable remaining in your wealth equation is you. The formula for financial freedom has been solved and presented. Now it's time for you to plug in your own values and begin calculating your wealthy future. Your journey from financial struggle to financial sovereignty begins not someday but today, not somewhere but here, not with someone else but with you.

The path to wealth is no longer mysterious but mathematical. The question isn't whether you can build wealth, the mathematics prove you can. The question is whether you will. Your financial future awaits your decision. Choose wealth. Choose freedom. Choose to begin.

Your journey to financial independence starts now.

## Your Special You Will Rock! Parting Gift

As a way of saying *thank you* for investing in this book, and for choosing to think differently about money, we're including an exclusive bonus resource designed to help you move from insight to action.

Understanding the rules of money is powerful. Applying them is what changes everything. This bonus exists to help bridge that gap by giving you practical tools you can use immediately, without complexity or guesswork.

**Inside this resource, you'll find:**

• Key money rules most people never learn, and how to apply them in real life

• Common financial mistakes that quietly keep people stuck (and how to avoid them)

• Small habit shifts that compound into massive financial results over time

• Clear next steps you can take right now, regardless of your current income or starting point

**Scan the QR code below** to unlock your exclusive bonus resource and start putting the rules of money to work for you today.

# BIBLIOGRAPHY

## PERSONAL FINANCE AND WEALTH BUILDING

Clason, George S. *The Richest Man in Babylon*. New York: Penguin, 1926.

Hill, Napoleon. *Think and Grow Rich*. Meriden: The Ralston Society, 1937.

Kiyosaki, Robert. *Rich Dad Poor Dad*. Paradise Valley: TechPress, 1997.

Stanley, Thomas J., and William D. Danko. *The Millionaire Next Door*. Atlanta: Longstreet Press, 1996.

Bach, David. *The Automatic Millionaire*. New York: Broadway Books, 2004.

Sethi, Ramit. *I Will Teach You to Be Rich*. New York: Workman Publishing, 2009.

Robbins, Tony. *Money: Master the Game*. New York: Simon & Schuster, 2014.

Housel, Morgan. *The Psychology of Money*. Petersfield: Harriman House, 2020.

## INVESTMENT STRATEGY

Graham, Benjamin. *The Intelligent Investor*. New York: Harper & Brothers, 1949.

Bogle, John C. *The Little Book of Common Sense Investing*. Hoboken: John Wiley & Sons, 2007.

Malkiel, Burton. *A Random Walk Down Wall Street*. New York: W.W. Norton, 1973.

Lynch, Peter. *One Up On Wall Street*. New York: Simon & Schuster, 1989.

Bernstein, William. *The Four Pillars of Investing*. New York: McGraw-Hill, 2002.

Siegel, Jeremy. *Stocks for the Long Run*. New York: McGraw-Hill, 1994.

Swensen, David. *Unconventional Success*. New York: Free Press, 2005.

Ellis, Charles D. *Winning the Loser's Game*. New York: McGraw-Hill, 1985.

## REAL ESTATE

Keller, Gary. *The Millionaire Real Estate Investor*. New York: McGraw-Hill, 2005.

Turner, Brandon. *The Book on Rental Property Investing*. BiggerPockets Publishing, 2015.

McElroy, Ken. *The ABCs of Real Estate Investing*. Paradise Valley: RDA Press, 2004.

Greene, David. *Buy, Rehab, Rent, Refinance, Repeat*. BiggerPockets Publishing, 2019.

Poorvu, William J. *The Real Estate Game*. New York: Free Press, 1999.

## BUSINESS AND ENTREPRENEURSHIP

Gerber, Michael E. *The E-Myth Revisited*. New York: HarperBusiness, 1995.

Ries, Eric. *The Lean Startup*. New York: Crown Business, 2011.

Thiel, Peter. *Zero to One*. New York: Crown Business, 2014.

Guillebeau, Chris. *The $100 Startup*. New York: Crown Business, 2012.

Ferriss, Timothy. *The 4-Hour Workweek*. New York: Crown Publishers, 2007.

Horowitz, Ben. *The Hard Thing About Hard Things*. New York: Harper Business, 2014.

## BITCOIN AND CRYPTOCURRENCY

Nakamoto, Satoshi. "Bitcoin: A Peer-to-Peer Electronic Cash System." Bitcoin.org, 2008.

Antonopoulos, Andreas M. *Mastering Bitcoin*. Sebastopol: O'Reilly Media, 2014.

Ammous, Saifedean. *The Bitcoin Standard*. Hoboken: Wiley, 2018.

Vigna, Paul and Michael J. Casey. *The Age of Cryptocurrency*. New York: St. Martin's Press, 2015.

Popper, Nathaniel. *Digital Gold*. New York: Harper, 2015.

## PSYCHOLOGY AND BEHAVIORAL ECONOMICS

Kahneman, Daniel. *Thinking, Fast and Slow*. New York: Farrar, Straus and Giroux, 2011.

Ariely, Dan. *Predictably Irrational*. New York: HarperCollins, 2008.

Thaler, Richard H., and Cass R. Sunstein. *Nudge*. New Haven: Yale University Press, 2008.

Zweig, Jason. *Your Money and Your Brain*. New York: Simon & Schuster, 2007.

## TAX STRATEGY

Piper, Mike. *Taxes Made Simple*. Simple Subjects LLC, 2010.
Larson, Mark J. *Tax Deductions for Professionals*. Nolo Press, 2020.
Sutherland, J.K. *Wealth Building Tax Strategies*. American Bar Association, 2019.

## ESTATE PLANNING

Clifford, Denis. *Plan Your Estate*. Nolo Press, 2020.
Esperti, Robert A., and Renno L. Peterson. *Protect Your Estate*. New York: McGraw-Hill, 1999.
Shotwell, John T. *Pass It On*. New York: Hyperion, 2001.

## HISTORICAL AND ECONOMIC CONTEXT

Ferguson, Niall. *The Ascent of Money*. New York: Penguin Press, 2008.
Reinhart, Carmen M., and Kenneth Rogoff. *This Time Is Different*. Princeton: Princeton University Press, 2009.
Piketty, Thomas. *Capital in the Twenty-First Century*. Cambridge: Belknap Press, 2014.
Taleb, Nassim Nicholas. *The Black Swan*. New York: Random House, 2007.
Dalio, Ray. *Principles for Navigating Big Debt Crises*. Bridgewater Associates, 2018.

**Important Disclosure and Disclaimer**

## THIS BOOK IS NOT FINANCIAL ADVICE

## NO PERSONALIZED RECOMMENDATIONS

The strategies, principles, and examples discussed in this book are general in nature and may not be suitable for your specific financial situation. Every individual's financial circumstances are unique, and the strategies that work for one person may not be appropriate for another. You should not rely on any information in this book as a substitute for individual advice from a qualified financial professional who is aware of your specific circumstances.

## CONSULT PROFESSIONAL ADVISORS

Before making any financial decisions or implementing any strategies discussed in this book, you should consult with qualified professionals, including but not limited to:

- Certified Financial Planners (CFP)
- Certified Public Accountants (CPA)
- Licensed Investment Advisors
- Estate Planning Attorneys
- Tax Professionals
- Insurance Agents
- Real Estate Professionals

These professionals can provide personalized advice based on your individual financial situation, goals, risk tolerance, and time horizon.

## INVESTMENT RISKS

All investments carry risk, including the potential loss of principal. Past performance does not guarantee future results. The investment returns mentioned in this book are historical examples or mathematical illustrations and should not be considered as promises or guarantees of future performance. Markets can be volatile, and you should be prepared for the possibility of losing money on any investment.

## NO GUARANTEES

While this book presents mathematical principles and historical data, there is no guarantee that following the strategies outlined will result in financial gain. Economic conditions, market dynamics, regulatory environments, and individual circumstances can all affect outcomes. The authors and publishers make no representations or warranties about the accuracy, completeness, or suitability of the information contained in this book.

## CRYPTOCURRENCY AND ALTERNATIVE INVESTMENTS

Discussions of Bitcoin, cryptocurrencies, and other alternative investments are particularly speculative and volatile. These assets carry substantial risk of loss and may not be suitable for all investors. The regulatory environment for these assets is evolving and uncertain. You should conduct thorough research and consider your risk tolerance carefully before investing in any cryptocurrency or alternative investment.

## TAX AND LEGAL CONSIDERATIONS

Tax laws and regulations are complex and subject to change. The tax strategies discussed in this book may not apply to your situation and could change based on new legislation or regulations. Always consult with a qualified tax professional before implementing any tax strategy. Similarly, legal strategies such as estate planning and asset protection should only be implemented with the guidance of qualified legal counsel.

## REAL ESTATE RISKS

Real estate investments carry unique risks including but not limited to market risk, liquidity risk, leverage risk, and management risk. The real estate strategies discussed in this book may require significant capital, time, and expertise. Local market conditions, regulations, and economic factors can significantly impact real estate investments.

## BUSINESS RISKS

Starting or operating a business involves substantial risk, including the potential for total loss of investment. Most new businesses fail within the first five years. The business strategies discussed in this book are not guaranteed to succeed and should be thoroughly researched and planned before implementation.

## INDIVIDUAL RESPONSIBILITY

You are solely responsible for your financial decisions and their consequences. The authors, publishers, and any affiliated parties assume no responsibility or liability for any losses or damages you may incur as a result of using the information in this book. By reading this book, you acknowledge that you are solely responsible for your own financial decisions.

## ACCURACY OF INFORMATION

While every effort has been made to ensure the accuracy of the information in this book at the time of publication, the authors and publishers make no representations or warranties about the accuracy, reliability, completeness, or timeliness of the information. Financial information, tax laws, and regulations change frequently, and some information in this book may become outdated.

## THIRD-PARTY INFORMATION

This book may reference third-party products, services, or strategies. These references are for informational purposes only and do not constitute endorsements or recommendations. The authors and publishers are not responsible for the content, products, or services of any third parties mentioned in this book.

## GEOGRAPHIC LIMITATIONS

The strategies and information in this book are primarily based on United States financial systems, tax laws, and regulations. If you reside outside the United States, many of the strategies discussed may not apply or may need significant modification. Always consult with local professionals familiar with your country's financial and legal environment.

## CONFLICTS OF INTEREST

The authors and publishers may have financial interests in some of the strategies, products, or services mentioned in this book. These potential conflicts of interest do not constitute recommendations, and you should evaluate all strategies independently based on your own circumstances.

## EARNINGS DISCLAIMERS

Any earnings or income examples mentioned in this book are illustrative only and should not be considered as typical or guaranteed results. Your results will vary based on numerous factors including but not limited to your starting capital, effort, market conditions, and individual capabilities.

## FINAL NOTICE

BY READING THIS BOOK, YOU ACKNOWLEDGE THAT YOU HAVE READ AND UNDERSTOOD THIS DISCLAIMER AND AGREE TO BE BOUND BY ITS TERMS. IF YOU DO NOT AGREE WITH THESE TERMS, YOU SHOULD NOT USE THE INFORMATION CONTAINED IN THIS BOOK.

Remember: Your financial future is your responsibility. Use this book as education and inspiration, but always make financial decisions based on professional advice tailored to your specific situation.

*The Millionaire Upstairs* is intended to educate and inspire, not to provide specific personal financial guidance. Your path to financial independence will be unique to your circumstances. Take what serves you from these pages, adapt it to your situation with professional guidance, and create your own mathematical certainty of wealth. Some of these stories are fictional, to be used as examples only.